When Sol went up to lift the FA Cup

The ⚓ News

at heart ♡ publications
www.atheart.co.uk

First published in 2008 by
At Heart Ltd
32 Stamford Street
Altrincham
Cheshire
WA14 1EY

in conjunction with
The News
The News Centre
Hilsea
Portsmouth
PO2 9SX

Words by Jordan Cross.

Pictures by Paul Jacobs, Will Caddy, Steve Reid, Ian Hargreaves, Malcolm Wells, Michael Scaddan and Allan Hutchings.

ISBN: 978-1-84547-212-2

Printed and bound by Bell & Bain, Glasgow.

CONTENTS

FOREWORD

What a great season.

I'm so glad we can all look back on what we achieved with so much pride. To win the FA Cup for the first time in 69 years – what an achievement.

Lifting the famous old trophy was something I dreamed about as a boy – we all do. And now we can say we did it. It was not just about winning the Cup, though. The scenes afterwards were unbelievable. Seeing all those people at Wembley so happy just leaves a lump in your throat.

The following day's parade through the city's streets was something else, too – such a special time for everybody connected with this football club.

I remember the parade back in 2003, when we won promotion to the Premier League, and that was fantastic. But this time was far, far bigger than that. It seemed everyone in the city was lining the streets to cheer us on and their reaction was fully appreciated. It proves what special supporters we have here, but we knew that anyway. Now the world can see for itself how tremendous our fans are.

Then it was on to Southsea Common where I think 200,000 people came out to attend. That really was exceptional. To see all those people in one place at the same time was truly mind blowing and capped a great, great day. It meant an awful lot to us and I know for a fact everyone on that bus and on that stage will never forget it. The whole thing was brilliant.

Since I've been here we've kept on progressing and as a manager that's what you really want to achieve. It's step by step. We won the First Division title in the first year and then stayed up in the second – our first year in the Premier League.

I know I left the year after but even then the club was in a good state with us in a decent League position. Then I came back halfway through the campaign and we stayed up with that tremendous end to the season.

Now here we are – FA Cup winners, eighth in the Premier League and in Europe. We've got some fantastic players here, but this season is definitely better than I ever imagined. Now we'll be looking ahead to our first-ever season in Europe and building for the future.

These are great times for this club. And it's nothing more than our fantastic supporters deserve.

Harry Redknapp
Manager, Portsmouth FC

INTRODUCTION

Who would have thought it?

Who would ever have believed on Sunday, December 2, 2007, when Pompey were given a seemingly innocuous assignment in the third round of the FA Cup, such glory lay in wait? Who would have ever considered that ex-Ipswich Town star Kevin Beattie would help pair the club he made his name at with Harry Redknapp's heroes, and would be the catalyst for something so special?

It was that very draw which sparked a rumpus as former Arsenal defender Sammy Nelson appeared to incorrectly announce a ball number. Fast forward 168 days and football's famous, old trophy had everyone talking about a very different story. The tale of a team restoring the romance to the biggest, most historic, most enthralling domestic club competition on the planet made the world stand up and take notice. The chronicle of a team captivating a city and giving their people an overflowing sense of pride. The voyage which ended in 200,000 fans paying homage to the men who made it possible in unprecedented scenes, which are unlikely to ever be equalled again.

Nobody knew where the journey would take us, as David Nugent grabbed the definitive strike, and the colossus that is David James made save after save to repel a late Ipswich onslaught on a chilly Suffolk afternoon in January. No one truly understood just how significant it would be that Lassana Diarra and Niko Kranjcar – two of the heroes of the day of reckoning – would overturn plucky Plymouth's early lead in the fourth round. And those who stood up to the crisp Deepdale cold to watch their men withstand a second-half firestorm from Preston before seizing an unlikely fifth-round victory, still would never have predicted the final outcome.

Throughout history, Pompey supporters have been forced to believe in their team through adversity. That's what has kept them steadfast through dark chapters in their club's past. A lifetime has passed since Jimmy Guthrie walked the 39 steps to receive football's famous old trophy from King George VI from the Royal Box in 1939. It was 69 long years since the mighty Wolves were sent packing by Jack Tinn's heroes, after being thumped 4-1 at the Empire Stadium.

Just as those with blue blood pumping through their veins began to dream it could happen again, a monolithic barrier was placed before them to test their resolve to the limit. A trip to the Champions, where no man wearing the star and crescent had triumphed for 51 years, was enough to challenge the faith of the most fervent of followers. Yet believe they did, and when Sulley Muntari stepped up at the Theatre of Dreams the fantasy became palpable. That ensured the moment so many thought they would never witness came true, Pompey walking out at Wembley for their semi-final date with West Brom.

The Blue Army descending on the home of football was a sight to behold, a day to cherish. Kanu's strike against his old side gave Pompey the chance to join the greats. And so it came to pass. On a day that will be forever embedded in the hearts of every member of their faithful, Redknapp and his men became immortals.

Portsmouth Football Club: FA Cup winners 2008. A kaleidoscope of colour, a blur of different images, emotions and memories from this pilgrimage will endure forever. Now sit back and relive that journey. Over and over again.

ROUND THREE

IPSWICH 0   POMPEY 1

FA Cup third-round day – one of the most exciting on the football calendar. Always an upset, always plucky underdogs emerging victorious and embodying exactly what the grandest and most famous of club competitions is all about. And those looking for a story had their eyes trained on Portman Road to deliver the result to grab the headlines. Experts and pundits were lining up to tip Pompey's trip to Ipswich as a potential Premier League banana skin.

The tournament was littered with the carcasses of established, powerful outfits who had fallen at this stage, and to lesser sides than Jim Magilton's well-schooled Tractor Boys. It's true the tie had the hallmarks of a match which could have got some serious air time on Match of the Day, as the big boys came unstuck. A Championship side who had failed to see defeat on their own patch all season, welcoming Harry Redknapp's patched-up outfit. Pompey went into the game off the back of a New Year's Day win at Reading which had lifted spirits after their worst run of the season.

Defeats to Spurs, Liverpool and Middlesbrough enveloped a backs-to-the-wall 0-0 draw with Arsenal on Boxing Day. The goals which were flowing freely as the Blues established themselves as European contenders in the league were beginning to dry up. Just one had arrived in the previous four games, before John Utaka and Sol Campbell ensured all three points were harvested at the Madejski Stadium. That meant

firepower was at the top of Redknapp's agenda with the shutters raised on the January transfer window. David Nugent, still looking for his first Premier League goal, had failed to provide the answers following his high-profile summer arrival from Preston.

Redknapp was keen to get to work on his shopping list, and the word was that this could mean some established first-team names being sacrificed to action those arrivals. Speculation linking fans' favourite Matt Taylor with a move away from Pompey had reached fever pitch, with Bolton and Reading said to be among his many suitors. His departure appeared to be closer than ever after Redknapp left him out of his already creaking squad with his 'mind not on the game'. With Sean Davis, Richard Hughes, Jamie Ashdown, Martin Cranie and Linvoy Primus also missing, Redknapp's roster – to coin his oft-used phrase – was down to the bare bones. Those injuries meant there was little chance to rest other established names. It was just as well, too.

Nugent may rarely have looked like delivering in the League, but he was proving something of a Cup talisman, with two goals in as many Carling Cup appearances. Redknapp was to turn to the Scouser as a second-half substitute to finally unlock plucky Ipswich. But it would prove to be the performance of a man at the other end of the pitch, the man the fans knew as 'England's number one', which would ultimately secure Pompey's passage into the fourth round.

SPORT FOCUS

Muntari & Co plan explosive exit

I'M GOING TO SIGN OFF IN STYLE

Ipswich is Sulley Muntari's last game for Pompey before the African Cup of Nations in Ghana

PICTURE: STEVE REID

by Neil Allen
Chief sports writer

SULLEY MUNTARI is eyeing an Ipswich swansong as he bids to go out with an African Nations bang.

The all-action midfielder will tomorrow wave goodbye to Pompey after their FA Cup trip to link-up with Ghana.

Papa Bouba Diop, Kanu and John Utaka will join him jetting out of England on Sunday to meet with their respective countries.

The players will be away from Pompey duty until their sides are knocked out of the competition.

With the African Cup of Nations final scheduled on February 10, several of the quartet could be missing for five Blues matches plus a prospective FA Cup fourth-round fixture.

For the time being ,though, Muntari is concentrating on fulfilling his club duties against Ipswich and firing Pompey into the next round.

And he admits he'll be leaving with a heavy heart.

He said: 'It's definitely difficult to leave your club side at this moment but you can't do anything about it. It's in the rules so I have to leave.

'It's like playing good music and your momma stops the music. We are playing very well and I am enjoying it.

'We have a great atmosphere and want to get into Europe, that is something I think we can achieve.

'It's going to be sad but I can't do anything, I have to represent my country because they made me who I am today.

'Without them people would not see me around.

'To represent your country is amazing and I will be very, very proud.

'It won't be the end of Portsmouth, though. There are players who can fill in and I know the manager will be able to make them play.

'I believe Portsmouth will be fine.

'I don't think it will be difficult for them without us, there are some very good players here.

'I will be sad to go, though.'

Muntari will attend a Ghana training camp ahead of their January 20 opener against Guinea.

As hosts, his side are ranked as one of the favourites to take the competition, while Kanu and Utaka's Nigeria are also highly regarded.

And the 23-year-old is relishing the chance to compete in the prestigious tournament.

He added: 'It's going to be great, the fans are ready for the African Cup of Nations.

'It's going to be one of the best. The African Cup is only one continent but it's watched by everyone in the world now.

'It's competitive, has good players around and produces very good football. It's going to be huge.'

Rangers lead the chase for Taylor

POMPEY'S Matt Taylor has emerged as a prime target for Rangers.

The Scottish giants are desperate for an attacking left-back and the out-of-favour 26-year-old fits the bill perfectly.

Harry Redknapp has already admitted he will listen to offers for Taylor, who has struggled to break into the first team this season.

The ex-Luton man himself has conceded he will look to leave if the situation does not improve.

And with money to spend to strengthen their assault on the Scottish Premier title, Rangers are poised to make a move.

Boss Walter Smith has made finding a left-back a priority, having struggled to fill the role this season.

First-choice Steven Smith has been sidelined by injury for the campaign so far, while stand-ins Sasa Papac and Steven Whittaker have failed to impress.

Sources in Scotland have confirmed Taylor, *above*, is his preferred option.

His days at Pompey appeared to be numbered, having become a casualty of Redknapp's drive for Europe.

Previously a regular, Taylor has failed to start a league game since the 3-1 defeat at Arsenal at the start of September.

The former England under-21 international currently finds himself a permanent fixture on the Blues bench.

Now, after 203 appearances and 29 goals, Redknapp is preparing to let Taylor go but only for the right fee.

That has alerted the likes of Sunderland, Reading, Bolton Middlesbrough, Fulham and Everton. But chief executive Peter Storrie revealed he had yet to receive an approach.

He said: 'We have not had an enquiry for Matt at the moment so we will have to wait and see on that one.'

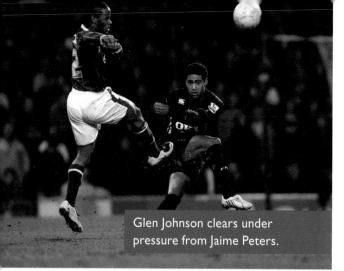
Glen Johnson clears under pressure from Jaime Peters.

IPSWICH 0 POMPEY 1 Cup specialist David Nugent struck again to see Pompey safely past ten-man Ipswich. The former Preston man may not have had a Premier League goal to his name, but it was an entirely different matter when it came to the knockout competitions. Entering the FA Cup clash at half-time, he latched on to Sol Campbell's pass to finish past Neil Alexander in the 51st minute. His third goal in four Cup appearances this season proved the difference as Pompey made hard work of beating an Ipswich side reduced to ten men.

Liam Trotter saw red in the 24th minute, following a two-footed lunge on Pedro Mendes. Yet it proved to be a controversial decision from referee Mark Halsey, with the youngster failing to make contact with the midfielder and appearing to warrant only a yellow. Not that it mattered too much to Ipswich, who still produced a spirited display. They could almost have snatched a replay in the dying minutes, with David James saving magnificently from substitute Alan Lee and Danny Haynes. Meanwhile, Nugent also hit the bar. But it was the one goal that proved the difference as Pompey safely moved into the fourth round.

Ipswich started brightly and had strangled calls for a penalty waved away in the fifth minute when David Wright crumpled under a challenge from Sylvain Distin. At the other end, Hermann Hreidarsson came so close to netting on his Portman Road return when he headed Niko Kranjcar's corner narrowly past the right-hand post. It was looking like an open affair and Glen Johnson ventured forward with a surging run past

three players before whipping in a low shot which was well parried at the near post by Neil Alexander. Ipswich then gave Pompey a real scare with a sweeping counter attack, which saw Billy Clarke dig out a deep cross that agonisingly just eluded the unmarked Haynes' burst into the box. On 12 minutes, Papa Bouba Diop wasted a golden opportunity to give his side the lead. John Utaka's inch-perfect cross from the right picked him out, but the Senegal midfielder failed to even test Alexander with his header from barely six yards out, the keeper gathering easily.

Ipswich were also having their moments and Distin's loose clearance provided Clarke with the opportunity to fire in a first-time effort which he screwed wide. The hosts were then reduced to ten men after a poor challenge by Trotter. The young midfielder lunged in with a two-footed tackle on Mendes, which had the Pompey player hurdling and referee Mark Halsey reaching for the red card. The decision shocked players from both sides and immediately lifted the crowd who

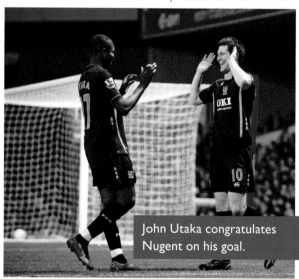
John Utaka congratulates Nugent on his goal.

made their disgust at the referee's decision known. It meant for the second away match running, Pompey had a numerical advantage early in the game. Ipswich fans had taken exception to Mendes following the decision, booing him every time he came into possession.

The atmosphere was rocking and, boosted by the additional man, even Sol Campbell took to marauding forward with the ball at his feet to exploit the space. And with Ipswich dropping Clarke into midfield to leave Pablo Counago as the lone striker, the

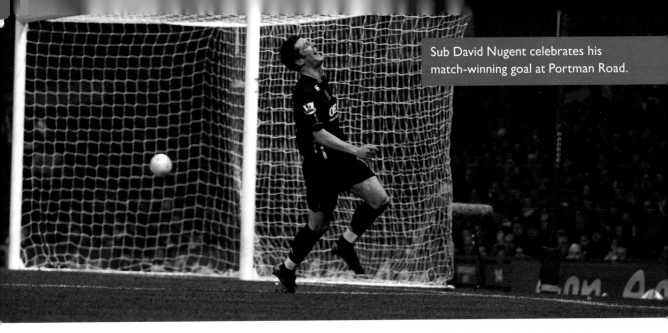

Pompey skipper could afford to be offensive. But the Tractor Boys were refusing to let Trotter's departure hinder them and were still looking threatening on the break. On 38 minutes, David James even had to venture outside his penalty area to clear under pressure from Clarke by the right-hand corner flag. Pompey lacked that killer instinct and in their latest attack, Diop blazed over from just outside the box following good work from Kanu. It prompted a rendition of 'Premier League? You're having a laugh' from the mocking Ipswich fans.

As the first half entered two minutes of stoppage time, Utaka wastefully blasted over from the angle after Kranjcar's excellent pass. Ipswich should have gone in at the interval in the lead, but Clarke saw his effort from two yards out brilliantly blocked by Johnson with the goal beckoning. Pompey made a half-time substitution, with Nugent replacing Mendes as Harry Redknapp reverted to a 4-4-2 formation. The former Preston man almost made an instant impact when a ball over the top down the left channel put him through, but Wilnis did well to stand firm and the chance was gone.

At the other end, Haynes came agonisingly close to netting for the hosts with a drive which James did superbly well to tip around the post. The deadlock was finally broken in the 50th minute with that man Nugent the scorer. Campbell's ball over the top released Nugent who took one touch before squeezing a shot under Alexander and into the net. As Pompey took

control of the match, Kranjcar crashed a right foot effort which Alexander did well to gather low down. On 59 minutes, Ipswich made their first substitution when Peters replaced Clarke in midfield. It was Pompey who came close to netting next, Nugent swivelling to send the ball crashing against the bar after good work from Utaka down the right. Ipswich were not done, though, and urged on by their vocal crowd they continued to threaten, with Haynes in particular impressing. Diop then wasted another great opportunity to record his maiden Pompey goal when he crashed the ball over from outside the box after being teed up by Kranjcar. Counago was booked for dissent on 70 minutes after being pulled up for a foul on Distin.

There were still goals left in Pompey and when Nugent twisted and turned his way into the Ipswich penalty area, he pulled the ball back for Kanu but the Nigerian struck his shot well over. Moments later, Johnson clipped in a brilliant free-kick from the right, only for Diop to see his goal-bound header superbly parried and then taken at the second opportunity by Alexander. Utaka then produced one of the misses of the season when he failed to tap home Hreidarsson's cross from the left from two yards out. Ipswich brought on Alan Lee for Williams to add extra firepower. Sure enough, the big striker produced a towering header on 83 minutes which had James brilliantly clawing out to keep Pompey's lead intact. James then had to produce a marvellous stoppage-time save from Haynes as Pompey clung on for victory.

KEY MAN
DAVID JAMES

Produced some late brilliant saves to prevent another FA Cup upset in a round of giant killings. The England shot-stopper delivered acrobatics to palm away Alan Lee's header. And he was back at his stunning best moments later with a fingertip save to deny Danny Haynes' fierce drive.

David James pulls off another save from a point-blank header by Jaime Peters.

Papa Bouba Diop challenges Pablo Counago in the air.

Niko Kranjcar brings the ball out of defence.

Sol Campbell beats Pablo Counago to the ball.

Goalscorer David Nugent takes on Fabian Wilnis.

Kanu closes down
Fabian Wilnis.

THIRD-ROUND SUMMARY

Pompey may have avoided their banana skin at Ipswich, but a host of other Premier League teams fell at the third-round stage. And Havant and Waterlooville helped bring romance back to the FA Cup, as they dumped out League One leaders Swansea. Shaun Gale's men grabbed the most unlikely of 1-1 draws in a stormy clash at the Liberty Stadium. But that was nothing compared to their sensational 4-2 win in the replay, on a night to remember at West Leigh Park.

That was far from the only shock as a string of top flight sides were dumped out. Fulham, Bolton,

Blackburn and Everton were all turned over by lower-league opposition. Blackburn were thumped 4-1 at home by Coventry in one of the performances of the round, while League One side Oldham triumphed at Everton. Fulham eventually succumbed on the mud at Bristol Rovers on penalties, Sheffield United were victorious at Bolton's Reebok Stadium, and Liverpool needed a replay before finally defeating Luton Town. Cardiff had to come from behind to avoid losing to the smallest club ever to reach the third round: Southern League division one midlands minnows, Chasetown, held a 1-0 advantage until the stroke of half-time, before going down 3-1.

The News

monday
sport
07.01.2008

David Nugent celebrates his 51st-minute goal with John Utaka at Portman Road
PICTURE: STEVE REID

Striker sees off Ipswich and keeps Pompey's FA Cup dream alive

NICE ONE NUGE

The News SPORT

James: No ref justice... why Taylor was left out... Hawks joy... rugby... local results

sport

Contact the sports desk on (023) 9266 4488 | E-mail: sport@thenews.co.uk | www.portsmouth.co.uk

NICE ONE NUGE

SPORT FOCUS

CHAMP OF THE DAY
STEFFI SMEE
Seagull darts star in last tour of world event after beating number one of her career

CHUMP OF THE DAY
ROBERTO MARTINEZ
Bananas boss slammed Hawks' rough tactics – his side should toughen up

WHAT THEY SAID
'I want to get fit and be fit for Mr Capello's first game'
David Beckham on the new England regime

YOUR VOTE

Today's question
Is David Nugent ready to be a regular starter up front for Pompey?

Vote by logging on to www.portsmouth.co.uk and click Pompey Pages

49%

In the weekend's web poll said Sol Campbell should be Pompey's number-one priority in the transfer window.
☐ 22% want Kei Andrea
☐ 20% thought Peter Crouch should be top choice.
☐ 5% chose someone else.
☐ 2% called for Jonas Gutierrez to be signed up.
☐ 1% said Bobby Zamora was the best choice.

POLE POSITION CLASSIFIEDS

It's party time yet again for the Hawks as club players and officials celebrate their 1-1 draw against Swansea at the Liberty Stadium
PICTURE: JANE HAWES

KEEP IT UP
by Neil Allen
Chief sports writer

Harry issues challenge to Nugent and vows to give Cup hero a chance

Hawks hopeful big Cup tie will be on home soil
by Steve Wilson
The News

The News, 7 January 2008.

The News
Sports Mail
40p

The weekly newspaper for fans and players alike

PICTURE: STEVE REID

Saturday, January 5, 2008

IPSWICH 0
POMPEY 1
David Nugent 51
Att: 23,448

NU START

...takes claim for league chance with a timely Cup winner

Family affair for Sulley PAGE 5
Hermann defends Utaka form PAGE 7
What's the latest craze at training? PAGE 9

fans' respect PAGE 4

HAWKS ARE CUP HEROES YET AGAIN

ROUND FOUR

POMPEY 2 PLYMOUTH 1

A home tie with a lower-league opponent was Harry Redknapp's fourth-round desire. The Monday afternoon draw at Soho Square granted that wish in the shape of Championship side Plymouth Argyle. But more fundamental to Pompey's Cup hopes, and their future dreams, was Redknapp answering supporters' prayers with the news they wanted to hear.

Little did anyone know the drama that would ensue in the days following victory over Ipswich. That came to light only when talk of Newcastle's desire to see Redknapp succeed Sam Allardyce, and their confidence in making that happen, emerged. The news sent a seismic shockwave through Fratton Park and the city. The story gripped the football world as Redknapp agonised over whether to take on the task of rejuvenating the fortunes of one of England's biggest clubs.

Everything pointed to him taking up the post, until a Friday night meal with family prompted his decision to remain on the south coast. Redknapp cited his happiness at Pompey and quality of life on the south coast with his wife Sandra, as the key to rejecting the Toon's overtures. All of Pompey rejoiced at the news, but the gravity and exhausting nature of the saga meant the trip to Sunderland paled into insignificance as Pompey succumbed on Wearside.

Better was to follow, as hapless Derby provided the perfect cannon fodder as Fratton Park celebrated Redknapp's decision to stay with a 3-1 victory the following week. Benjani's second hat-trick of the season did for Paul Jewell's rock-bottom side, to ensure there was a feel-good air in the sea-breeze ahead of former Southampton boss Paul Sturrock's men's visit. That upbeat mood was further supplemented by the arrival of French international Lassana Diarra from Arsenal. Diarra had grown impatient at his bit-part role at the Emirates, allowing Redknapp to serenade the midfielder and secure his £5m capture. Redknapp insisted only time would show just what a huge coup Diarra's capture would prove to be. But his signing prompted a big enough fanfare to ensure left-back Lucien Aubey's loan move from Lens slipped largely under the radar. Matt Taylor's £3.5m switch to Bolton financed the bulk of Diarra's fee, as the man who had played such a huge role in making Pompey a Premier League force waved goodbye to the fans who adored him.

Redknapp had been typically active in the transfer market, but there was still no sign of the added weight up front he was looking for. There was still time for a few twists and turns before the window slammed shut at the end of January though.

First Pompey faced Plymouth in the match being billed as the 'Battle of the Ports'. It was a clash which was to again underline the importance of the Blues having a keeper feted as the best in the business between the sticks. And it would offer the stage for Diarra to show why he had never been a loser in 22 previous knockout games, spanning the Champions League, Carling Cup and FA Cup, since arriving in English football.

Win is vital for flagging Gosport
■ Page 66

Redknapp aims for Wembley
■ Page 70-71

Contact the sports desk on (023) 9266 4488　E-mail: sport@thenews.co.uk　www.portsmouth.co.uk

Pompey hope to sign Czech striker Milan Baros on loan for the rest of the season

BAROS CAN FIRE US INTO EUROPE

by Jordan Cross
The News

HARRY REDKNAPP has pinpointed Milan Baros as the man to take Pompey into Europe.

The Blues were today hoping to complete the loan signing of the Czech Republic hitman from French giants Lyon until the end of the season.

Redknapp feels the 26-year-old is the man with the clinical eye for goal his team have been missing.

The Pompey boss sees the former European Championship golden boot winner's capture as yet another major transfer coup.

He will weigh up Baros over the remainder of the season before deciding whether to make his stay at Fratton Park permanent.

Redknapp said: 'We are hoping to do something, we are hoping to loan him.

'Peter Storrie was talking to him yesterday.

'He went off to meet with his agent to try to do a deal.

'If he can put a deal together we will take him on loan.

'He's a good player, he's played at Liverpool and Aston Villa.

Harry's keen to wrap up deal for front man

'He won the golden boot one year at the European Championships.

'He's got pace and makes good runs.

'He'll be a good loan signing. It's a terrific opportunity to have him here and have a good look at him.

'He's at a big club, Lyon's a terrific club, and he's not getting in the side.

'They've got fantastic strikers.

'The boy Fred can't get in the team, he's 15-16m Euros to buy.

'Tottenham have tried to buy him as he can't get in the team.

'They are overloaded with so many good strikers.'

Redknapp expects to wind down Pompey's transfer activity with Baros' capture.

The only way he expects to splash out any significant cash is if he agrees a deal to move on any fringe players for major money.

Redknapp believes there still could be another short-term deal in the offing.

He has been keeping tabs on Arsenal's prodigious talent Theo Walcott (below) but doesn't expect him to be leaving the Emirates, despite talk of a loan move.

The Blues boss admitted he was interested in Watford's Marlon King, but feels that is now unlikely to happen.

Redknapp said: 'I think that would be more or less it unless I took another loan or one more short-term deal.

'I certainly wouldn't see us spending anymore money unless someone came in and offered us silly money for someone that wasn't in my team.

'Arsenal are not going to loan out Theo Walcott. I know they are not going to loan him.

'He's a good player Theo, terrific player, but they won't loan him.

'I was interested in Marlon King but I think Wigan and Fulham are in for him.'

Gale: We can cause the biggest upset ever

by Steve Wilson
The News

SHAUN GALE issued a rallying call to his troops ahead of the biggest FA Cup mismatch of all time and insisted: We can beat Liverpool.

The Hawks are all set for their daunting trip to Anfield with a massive 112 places separating the teams in the football pyramid and staggering odds of 100/1 against the West Leigh Park outfit pulling off what would surely be the greatest shock in FA Cup history.

But the Hawks boss has refused to accept his side will be on the receiving end of an Anfield battering and honestly believes an upset is possible.

Gale said: 'Anything is possible in football and miracles can happen.

'People buy lottery tickets every week and someone always wins.

'So let's just say we've bought our ticket.

'We all know that if Liverpool play fantastically well and we play fantastically well, there is only one winner.

Shaun Gale

'But if Liverpool don't play so well and we are at the very top of our game, anything can happen.

'There is no doubt Liverpool are one of the biggest sides in the world – and I'm sure they will be quaking in their boots at playing us!

'But all you can ask of the players is they go out and give their all.

'I'm sure they will.'

Gale's final preparations included spending time at Pompey's training ground yesterday using the Prozone analysis system to try to counter Liverpool.

And he believes whatever happens, the Hawks have put the magic back in the Cup.

Gale said: 'If there was any doubt about the FA Cup losing its appeal, I'd like to think we've re-ignited the FA Cup this season – especially for the non-league circuit.'

POMPEY 2 PLYMOUTH 1   Pompey kept their FA Cup hopes alive with a narrow victory over a dangerous Plymouth. This was no walk in the park on a Saturday afternoon for Harry Redknapp's men against the Championship outfit. Instead, the Blues were made to battle all the way for a 2-1 triumph to reach the fifth round of the FA Cup..

Plymouth debutant Chris Clark even prompted thoughts of an upset with a fifth-minute lead for Paul Sturrock's side. But Pompey hit back in the first half, with Lassana Diarra's first goal for the club when he drove home from distance on 34 minutes. And Niko Kranjcar weighed in with the all-important winner from close range on the stroke of half-time with a calm finish. But rather like their last-round victory against Ipswich, they were again indebted to David James on occasions who produced some marvellous saves. And the visitors were unfortunate not to get a late penalty after Rory Fallon's shot hit Sylvain Distin's left arm. Referee Andre Marriner instead awarded a corner. Pompey were even forced to employ just one striker up front in the second half after a groin injury to David Nugent. It may have dulled their creativity but it helped give them a grip on the game against the dangerous Pilgrims. And it was Redknapp's men who

won the battle of the naval dockyards to progress.

The Plymouth fans packed out the entire Milton End and generated a cracking pre-match Cup atmosphere. And they cranked up the noise level after just five minutes when they took a shock lead. Sylvain Distin produced a crunching block tackle on David Norris, the ball ricocheting to the unmarked Clark on the right. The former Aberdeen man took one touch before unleashing a shot which took a slight deflection off Hermann Hreidarsson and past David James into the net for the opener. Moments later, the visitors almost made it two when Rory Fallon collected Gary Sawyer's pass and swivelled to fire in his shot which James did well to push past the post. From the resulting corner, Jermaine Easter's flying volley was again well saved by Pompey's busy keeper. The home side was all over the place and on 11 minutes, Pedro Mendes' loose ball cross field fell to Peter Halmosi, and the Hungarian cracked in a low effort which again had James sprawling.

News of Havant & Waterlooville's shock lead at Anfield filtered through at Fratton Park to at least take the fans' thoughts off the game in front of them. Good job, too, with Argyle looking comfortable and well capable of stretching their advantage. The away support even found time to gloat, chanting: 'Are you watching Ian Holloway?' – a dig at the boss who left them for Milan

Niko Kranjcar tries to bring the ball down.

Mandaric's Leicester City weeks earlier. But Pompey were far from out of it and Benjani should have done better when he was released down the right and cut into the box, yet tried to do too much rather than pass and the chance was gone.

On 21 minutes, Glen Johnson surged down the right and fired in a cross which agonisingly eluded David Nugent's far-post lunge by a matter of inches. Those efforts provided Pompey with the encouragement they needed as they steadily began to find a foothold in the game. Within minutes of the Hawks regaining the lead at Anfield, Pompey fans were themselves given good cause to cheer.

effort which was held by Luke McCormick. Pompey did take the lead, though, on 45 minutes when Johnson flighted in a cross from the right, Plymouth failed to clear and Kranjcar was there to calmly slot home. The fourth official indicated there was an additional two minutes to be played and as he did so, Benjani almost got on the end of a fine move started by Lauren. But as it was, Pompey headed in at the interval with the lead and one foot in the fifth round.

Redknapp made an enforced substitution at half-time with groin-injury victim Nugent replaced by Arnold Mvuemba. With no strikers on the bench, it meant Pompey had to revert to the 4-5-1 system which had

David James pulls off another great save.

On 34 minutes, Mendes and Kranjcar combined for a right-wing corner, with the former sliding the ball back to Diarra, who fizzed a first-time effort from 25 yards. It took a slight deflection but the destination was never in any doubt and Pompey had their equaliser. Halmosi then became the first player of the afternoon to be booked following a tug on Johnson who was beginning to cause him problems. At the other end, Plymouth again threatened when Fallon produced a sublime piece of skill, chesting the ball down and volleying a shot which James gathered at the second attempt.

The game was developing into a Cup cracker and Nugent took advantage of a Sawyer slip to drive in an

proven so successful away from Fratton Park. And it was the visitors who initially looked the most threatening in the opening exchanges of the half. First, Halmosi fired in a left-foot effort which James did well to beat out at the near post. Moments later, the keeper again had to come to the Blues' rescue when Norris poked a pass through to Easter which had to be diverted for a corner. Diarra then brought the crowd to life with a magnificent run past four Plymouth players into the area before his cross was cut out by McCormick.

Matthias Doumbe became the latest player to be booked after bodychecking Mvuemba as he attempted

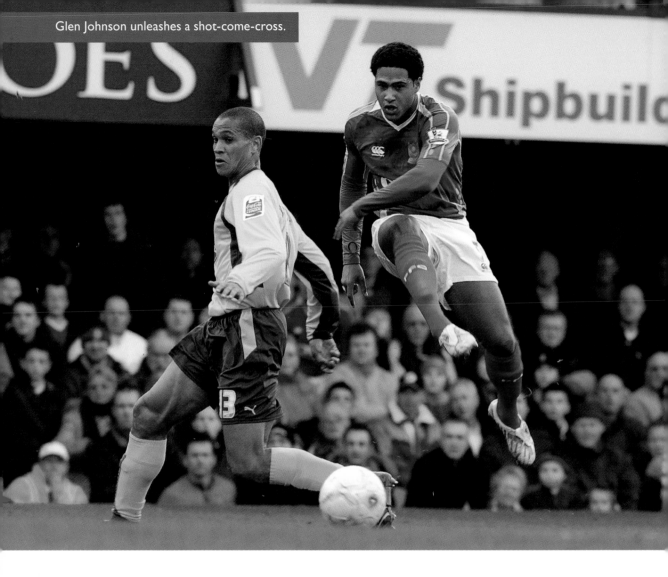

to surge by. Benjani then came agonisingly close to increasing the hosts' lead when he drilled in a shot from the right which flashed just past the far post. On 67 minutes, Pompey made their second substitution with Sean Davis introduced in favour of Lauren. Pompey may have had a fragile lead, but Plymouth still looked well capable of grabbing an equaliser with Halmosi in particular posing plenty of problems.

On 69 minutes, Clark's free-kick caused havoc in the Pompey penalty area and James had to show great reactions to thwart Fallon at close range. The Pilgrims' followers were now in fine vocal form as they attempted to spur their side on for the equaliser. Plymouth made their first substitution with Lucas

Jutkiewicz – on loan from Everton – replacing the lively Easter up front on 75 minutes. But Pompey were counting their blessings in the 79th minute when referee Marriner turned down strong appeals for a Pilgrims penalty. Fallon's shot appeared to clearly strike the left arm of Distin before bouncing away for a corner. Yet the match official infuriated the Plymouth following by instead granting a corner.

On 81 minutes, former Saints player Yoann Folly replaced goalscorer Clark. Mendes had the chance to wrap it all up with full-time approaching, but with just McCormick to beat he shot straight at the keeper. Pamarot was booked for encroaching after a foul on Halmosi. But Pompey were through.

KEY MAN
LASSANA DIARRA

Head and shoulders above everyone else on the pitch, the midfielder dazzled after recently signing from Arsenal. His range of passing and ability to grab the game by the scruff of the neck turned things around for the Blues. And to top it off, the Frenchman netted the crucial equaliser when Plymouth were threatening to spring a Cup shock.

Portsmouth's Lassana Diarra celebrates after scoring the second goal of the match.

Hermann Hreidarsson takes on Rory Fallon.

Distin (right) and Argyle's Jermaine Easter.

David Nugent narrowly misses a cross.

Lassana Diarra
bursting forward.

Pedro Mendes celebrates with Lassana Diarra after the French midfielder scores his first Pompey goal.

Benjani congratulates goalscorer Niko Kranjcar.

Pompey fans rejoice after Niko Kranjcar's winning goal.

FOURTH-ROUND SUMMARY

Havant and Waterlooville's brave FA Cup run came to an end, but not before they twice led at Liverpool. The Conference South side twice stunned Anfield through goals from Richard Pacquette and Alfie Potter, before eventually going down 5-2. It was a performance and run that captivated the nation and won hearts as the part-timers made a name for themselves.

'Balloongate' dominated the round as Sheffield United dumped out Sven-Goran Eriksson's Manchester City. Luton Shelton's opener in the 2-1 win came after Michael Ball failed to clear after the ball was diverted by balloons being thrown onto the pitch by City fans. Third round giantkillers Bristol Rovers, Huddersfield and Coventry all made it into the last 32. Manchester United flexed their muscle as they came from a goal behind to beat Spurs 3-1. Arsenal proved too strong for Newcastle as they cruised to a 3-0 win at the Emirates, while holders Chelsea knocked out Wigan at the JJB Stadium, winning 2-1. Cardiff ended Hereford's interest in the competition at Edgar Street. But the Bluebirds had to hold on, as the League Two side pulled a goal back with 14 minutes to go, before going down 2-1.

The News
Sports Mail

The weekly newspaper for fans and players alike

40p

Saturday, January 26, 2008

POMPEY 2
Diarra 34, Kranjcar 45
PLYMOUTH . . 1
Clark 5
Att: 19,612

Pompey are not at their best – but fight back to book place in the fifth round...
■ **Pages 2-3**

CUP HEROES

LIVERPOOL . . 5
Leiva 27, Benayoun 44, 56, 59, Crouch 90
HAWKS 2
Pacquette 8, Skrtel (og) 31
Att: 42,566

...Hawks give European giants Liverpool a real scare before bravely bowing out
■ **Pages 4-5**

9 770963 388309

ROUND FIVE

PRESTON 0 POMPEY 1

Harry Redknapp fully deserves his Houdini moniker for the number of magical tricks he has pulled off in his time at Pompey. But his 'Honest 'Arry, the wheeler dealer' tag is far less warranted when summing up his work in the transfer market. Redknapp is a proven top-drawer worker in that field, a man capable of coups to charm the players to power his team. Pompey fans were aware of that all right, but his deadline-day capture of England international Jermain Defoe from Spurs stretched even his previous brilliance to a new high.

Supporters looked on with disbelieving eyes as the race to snare the £7.5m hitman went up to, and eventually beyond, the midnight transfer window deadline on January 31. The ramifications of the move not being registered in time with the Premier League pen pushers would rumble on, before he was eventually secured permanently. Defoe was a deal to get supporters salivating but it was an astute piece of business at a price, as Benjani was sacrificed to action the move.

The Zimbabwean's 12 goals had attracted the interest of Manchester City, and Redknapp took the money on offer to finance Defoe. It was a no-brainer in the Pompey boss's eyes. It was a fantastic bit of business, but one which presented a blow to Pompey's FA Cup hopes. With Defoe cup-tied after appearing in the tournament for Spurs, it meant the clinical eye for goal he had already shown after scoring on his debut against Chelsea would be missing in the cup, and the fifth

round trip to Preston. The draw ensured a return to Deepdale for Redknapp, the place where it all started for him as Pompey manager. A 2-0 defeat marked his first game in charge as boss back in March, 2002. A lot of things had changed since then.

Other Premier League clubs had paid the price for not respecting the FA Cup by rolling out their full complement so far in the competition. Redknapp, however, had laid down a marker by fielding powerful sides for his two victories against Championship teams so far. That hadn't made success against Ipswich and Plymouth any easier to come by, though. A trip to Lancashire was clearly not going to be an easy obstacle to overcome either. Preston may have been toiling in the lower regions of the second tier, but a 4-1 thumping of Derby in the fourth round showed Pompey were not going to have it easy.

And so it was to prove. Pompey had developed the healthy habit of getting the job done so far, without being at their best. That had soaked through to their League form as they warmed up for the fifth round with a 1-0 victory at Bolton. Trotters boss Gary Megson bemoaned an archetypal smash and grab at the Reebok in the wake of his team's defeat.

But it was to pale in comparison to the hit-and-run job Alan Irvine's team were to suffer, as Pompey withstood their biggest, most concerted Cup onslaught yet, only to land the final concussive blow.

The News SPORT

Hawks keen to build on form — Page 54

Baros will be at his best — Page 58-59

Contact the sports desk on (023) 9266 4488 — E-mail: sport@thenews.co.uk — www.portsmouth.co.uk

SPORT FOCUS

CHAMP OF THE DAY

PAUL COLLINGWOOD
Inspirational captain's display as he quickled 70 not out handed England victory

CHUMP OF THE DAY

BRYAN ROBSON
Failed miserably in trying to get Sheffield United back in the top flight and has paid the price

WHAT THEY SAID

'It's time for trust. Ian has full support from all of us'

Milan Mandaric says he's happy with Ian Holloway.

YOUR VOTE

Today's question

How will Pompey get on in their FA Cup fifth-round clash at Preston?

Vote by logging on to www.portsmouth.co.uk and click Pompey Pages

63%

In yesterday's web poll said Niko Kranjcar's comments about his desire to one day play at the highest level should be expected from a player with ambition.

■ 16% thought it would have no effect on Pompey's bid for European football.

■ 11% felt Kranjcar deserved to sign for a major force.

■ 10% said the Croat's comments were a major blow.

Preston aim to give Nugent a tough time

PRESTON'S players have vowed not to give David Nugent a happy homecoming. And he's got the test messages to prove it.

The Pompey striker is back in the squad for Sunday's FA Cup clash with Preston after recovering from a hernia operation.

For Nugent, it's the chance to return to the club where he scored 35 goals in two-and-a-half seasons before his summer switch to the south coast.

The 22-year-old, however, is determined to place on the pitch...

UNLEASH THE DREAM TEAM

Redknapp is excited by pairing of Muntari and Diarra for Cup clash

by Neil Allen
Chief sports writer

HARRY REDKNAPP is set to unleash his midfield dream team on Preston.

The Blues boss reckons the mouth-watering pairing of Lassana Diarra and Sulley Muntari...

David Nugent

The News, 15 February 2008.

The News SPORT

Billy keeps his eye on the prize — Page 45

Pacquette's American Dream — Page 46

Contact the sports desk on (023) 9266 4488 — E-mail: sport@thenews.co.uk — www.portsmouth.co.uk

SPORT FOCUS

CHAMP OF THE DAY

ANDY MURRAY
Booked his place in the semi-finals.

Harry Redknapp will take nothing for granted against Preston

'ARRY READY TO ROLL OUT THE BIG GUNS

Redknapp to pay Championship side Preston utmost respect at Deepdale

by Steve Wilson
The News

HARRY REDKNAPP will resist the temptation to rest his top stars and will roll out the heavy artillery for tomorrow's FA Cup battle at Preston North End.

With six Premier League sides still left in the competition ahead of the fifth round...

Sulley Muntari (left) is set for a return

Pompey rubbish lingering Defoe talk

by Jordan Cross
The News

POMPEY have moved to bury lingering talk Jermain Defoe is not their player.

Speculation continues to circulate that Defoe is at Fratton Park on loan.

But the Blues revealed the striker's £7.5m move from Spurs was made permanent last week.

Jermain Defoe

The News, 16 February 2008.

The News Sports Mail

The weekly newspaper for fans and players alike

40p — Saturday, February 16, 2008

STORRIE HAILS HIS 'BEST-EVER' SIGNING

Full story ■ Pages 2-3

Is going global so bad? PAGE 4

I never gave up on England PAGE 5

The Cup remains so special PAGE 7

Fans have their say PAGE 6

WIN TICKETS TO POMPEY

Sports Mail, 16 February 2008.

Hermann Hreidarsson
celebrates Pompey's victory.

PRESTON 0 POMPEY 1   The FA Cup sat snugly in the confines of the Sky television box. Perched in front of the main window for a grandstand view of the Deepdale pitch, it provided a mouth-watering glimpse of what the future held for one of nine clubs. Not even that was going to be enough to keep Pompey's hands off it. It was written in the stars – and it appeared Portsmouth Football Club's name was written on the famous old trophy, too.

If Bolton's triumph was a smash and grab the week prior to this game, Preston was the scene of a brutal armed robbery brazenly carried out live on television. And when the Blues were in this mood there was nothing that could stop them. You couldn't helping feeling the Gods were on Pompey's side during their FA Cup campaign. And it had been too long coming. Harry Redknapp's side were fortunate to see off Ipswich, they were lucky to bundle out Plymouth. Here, they were downright lucky to edge past an excellent Preston outfit who, if there was any justice in this crazy world of ours, would have been anticipating FA Cup glory. Had it been a fight they would have won on points. Only this was too one-sided to even be classified as such – the matching was that unfair.

Ultimately, though, the knock-out blow was delivered by one of their own in the game's dying seconds, with not a Pompey player in the immediate vicinity. Icelandic warrior Hermann Hreidarsson pummelled the air in response, the relief only too apparent. He knew, and so did everyone who witnessed the 93 minutes which had unfolded, it was not deserved. Had it not been for that man-of-the-moment David James, Pompey would have been down and out long before the 93rd minute even kicked into action. A penalty stop and umpteen saves formed the backbone of a remarkable result for Redknapp and his troops. They not so much marched into the quarter-finals, rather stumbled battered, bloodied and somehow very much alive.

This was meant to be one of the kindest of draws, a trip to a side fighting for their Championship future and on their second manager of the season. In contrast, Pompey had travelled light years since Redknapp's first outing as boss at Deepdale back in March 2002. The likes of Mark Summerbell and Jamie Vincent lined up on that occasion. Nowadays, Summerbell reputedly runs a pub in Yorkshire while Vincent turns out for Swindon. A galaxy of stars have taken their places. Yet almost six years later, the result could have easily finished the same, with the home side taking the honours.

Not that the Blues boss had been caught out underestimating his opposition, no matter how sorry their season has become. In keeping with many of his managerial colleagues, Redknapp was not backwards in ringing the changes to the side. Except this was one example of FA Cup tinkering with the emphasis on strength. While the likes of Liverpool, Arsenal, Everton, Blackburn and co had meddled to their cost, the Blues boss fielded arguably the strongest XI at his disposal. Glen Johnson, Sulley Muntari, John Utaka, Sylvain Distin and Kanu were all given starting spots having sat out the Bolton triumph a week earlier. Not bad replacements considering four had been first-team regulars during the season, while the other was Pompey's joint-top scorer.

Elsewhere, injured duo Pedro Mendes and Noe Pamarot were obvious absentees, as was the cup-tied Jermain Defoe. Such were the riches at his disposal, there wasn't even a place on the bench for David Nugent and Sean Davis. The same duo were photographed enjoying a night out during the club's trip to Malaga weeks earlier. Those photographs had been emblazoned across the website of Lineker's Bar in Puerto Banus. However, the closest former Lilywhite Nugent got to the pitch was to draw the half-time raffle. The fixture was deemed a game too soon for his comeback following a hernia operation, while the surprise absence of Davis was credited as nothing more than tactical by Redknapp. Still, there was plenty of talent remaining to have comfortably crushed Preston. Well, on paper anyway. Reverting back to the 4-5-1

Lassana Diarra

system which had served so impressive away from home, the Blues welcomed back the counter-attacking talents of Utaka, the hold-up strengths of Kanu and the industry of African Cup of Nations star Muntari. Even lucky omen Diarra was in there, a player who had previously yet to be beaten in 23 games in domestic cup competition for Pompey, Chelsea and Arsenal. And, of course, England's best goalkeeper was occupying the goal and arguably in the form of his life. Surely nothing could go wrong?

The first half may have subsequently been dull but at least the visitors had their moments. Kanu steered a clever header from Johnson's raking ball which was dealt with comfortably by Andy Lonergan. Niko Kranjcar flashed a fierce drive over and then glanced a header from Muntari's cross into Lonergan's arms when he should have done better. Hermann Hreidarsson crashed the ball into the side netting while Kanu had strong appeals for a penalty turned away from Mike Dean after Youl Mawene appeared to handle twice. Come the second-half, though, Preston and their fans sensed an upset. They almost claimed first blood as well, when full-back Billy Jones was upended by Distin for a stone-wall penalty in the 59th minute. Winger Simon Whaley volunteered to take his first-ever North End spot kick – and James did the rest, flinging himself to his right to keep it out. From then on the hosts dominated as the James show took over, while his Pompey teammates wilted. There was a flying save

Milan Baros

from Chris Brown's long-ranger, a low stop to thwart Carter, and – the pick of the bunch – a brilliant fingertip save against substitute Neil Mellor.

How Pompey ached for the full-time whistle to at least take Preston back to Fratton Park for another go, their pride and goal still very much intact. But in the dying seconds, Kranjcar flighted in a corner from the left, chaos ensued before the ball finally crashed into the roof of the Preston net. Quite who the culprit was, no one knew. Then again, few connected with Pompey cared. Deepdale had been the crime scene of another piece of daylight robbery from Harry Redknapp and his Pompey gang. And who would have bet on the FA Cup itself also finding its way among their haul?

Hermann Hreidarsson shows his relief after an own goal from Preston's Darren Carter.

Sulley Muntari

Pompey's David James and Glen Johnson celebrate after the final whistle.

KEY MAN
DAVID JAMES

What more could have been said about this man? Having already kept Pompey in the Cup with a supershow in the third round win at Ipswich, he was once again the hero to deny a Preston onslaught. A penalty stop and a handful of top-drawer saves were decisive in sending Harry Redknapp's men through to the quarter-finals.

Papa Bouba Diop uses his head.

Kanu and Youl Mawene.

Sulley Muntari

Callum Davidson and Papa Bouba Diop.

Utaka challenges Preston's goalkeeper Andy Lonergan.

David James makes a penalty save.

The winning goal, an own goal by Preston's Darren Carter.

David James congratulates Papa Bouba Diop on the victory.

Sol Campbell celebrates.

John Utaka

Celebrating after a penalty save.

Lassana Diarra swerves past the Preston defence.

FIFTH-ROUND SUMMARY

Barnsley added their name to the burgeoning list of FA Cup giant killers as they stunned Liverpool at Anfield. Brian Howard's injury-time winner gave the lowly Championship side at 2-1 win over Rafa Benitez's men in the shock of the round. Stephen Foster had cancelled out Dirk Kuyt's opener, before Howard sent the Tykes fans into dreamland with seconds remaining. But the Yorkshire side weren't the only ones dumping out higher league opponents. Southampton became the latest team to fall victim to Bristol Rovers and their Memorial Ground swamp. Ricky Lambert celebrated his 26th birthday in style as his deflected 84th minute free-kick sent Pompey's hapless local rivals spinning out.

They were joined by Arsenal, who suffered an ominous 4-0 thumping at the hands of Manchester United. Sir Alex Ferguson could afford to leave Ryan Giggs and Cristiano Ronaldo out of his starting line-up and still trounce the Gunners. Wayne Rooney's virtuoso performance did the damage. He opened the scoring before two goals from Darren Fletcher and a Nani effort completed the romp. West Brom advanced to the quarter-finals with a 5-0 thrashing of Coventry. Middlesbrough needed a replay to account for Sheffield United and Chelsea defeated Huddersfield. Peter Whittingham and Jimmy-Floyd Hasselbaink gave Cardiff a 2-0 win over Wolves.

The News SPORT

James happy to nick win...
Davis axed for football reasons...
Happy Hawks... results

SMASH 'N' GRAB

Contact the sports desk on (023) 9266 4488 E-mail: sport@thenews.co.uk www.portsmouth.co.uk

SPORT FOCUS

WHAT THEY SAID

'I wouldn't call it a bad spell – it's been longer'

Jamie Carragher admits Liverpool are suffering more than just a 'bad spell'

YOUR VOTE

Today's question

Is David James the best goalkeeper in the Premier League?

Vote by logging on to www.portsmouth.co.uk and click Pompey Pages

59%

in the weekend's web poll said Pompey's wait for silverware would come to an end this year, with victory in the Cup.
■ 21% believed a place in the semi-final was all Pompey expect could expect.
■ 12% thought Pompey would be losing Cup finalists.
■ 5% reckoned the Blues' wait for a trophy would continue for another year.
■ 3% thought Pompey would have been beaten by Preston.

'ARRY: WE RODE OUR LUCK AT PRESTON

by Neil Allen
Chief sports writer

Pompey escape an FA Cup upset at Deepdale

Preston's Darren Carter stands dejected after his own goal with keeper Andy Lonergan

HARRY REDKNAPP hailed Pompey's 'bit of luck' after edging into the FA Cup's last eight.

The Blues were fortunate not to become the subject of yet another 2008 Cup upset after completing a smash-and-grab act at Preston.

Darren Carter's stoppage-time own goal settled a contest the visitors didn't deserve to emerge victorious from.

Redknapp's men rode their good fortune, during the second half especially, with David James producing another wonder show, including a penalty save from Simon Whaley.

Regardless, Pompey are now in the quarter-finals of the FA Cup for the first time since 2004.

But their boss afterwards held his hands up and admitted they had plenty of assistance in the good luck stakes to achieve it.

Redknapp said: 'I was waiting for the whistle to go and thinking let's get them back to Fratton Park.

'Then that happens. I didn't even know if it was an own goal.

'I asked Sol who put it over the line and he said it was an own goal. It doesn't matter, though, it's all over.

'You need a bit of luck sometimes and we've had a bit of luck up here the last two weeks to be fair.

'I said that after Bolton and again yesterday.

'It was a difficult game. I thought it was a difficult pitch to play on and it was difficult to get it down and really play.

'What they did well was they were willing up front, they had a bit of pace, they ran into channels, they got it forward and it suited them more than it did us, that's for sure.

'I think they were excellent, they were lively as well.

'List... thinks Preston an eas... understa... not been...

'It doe... Cup tie.

'I've be... of them...

'I've been to places like Swansea and Wrexham and got beaten, we knocked out Manchester United at Bournemouth when we were struggling at the bottom of the third division.

'At the end of the day, it's amazing what happens.

'I knew coming here would be a real tough Cup tie for us.'

Arsenal ended Pompey's last foray into the...

Redknapp insists James is staying put

by Neil Allen
Chief sports writer

HARRY REDKNAPP today promised Pompey fans: Jamo's going nowhere.

The England number one was this week linked with a shock move to Spurs as his sizzling form continues.

Juande Ramos is reportedly keen to replace the struggling Paul Robinson with the 37-year-old at the end of the season.

James shrugged off the rumours to once again put in an inspired display, including a penalty save, in Pompey's 1-0 Preston win yesterday.

His heroics helped extend an FA Cup run to the last eight as Pompey look towards a tantalising trip to Wembley.

And Redknapp has insisted his star man will not be going anywhere.

He said:
'Jamo's got another couple of years left here, I only gave him a new contract last year.

'I saw something in the paper that at the end of the year Tottenham are going to sign him – I don't think so.

'Where the reporter got that one from I don't know.

'Jim Smith must have told him that when they were having a glass of red wine. I couldn't believe it – where's he got that story from?

'He's under contract here and has another two years after this.

'I said to Peter Storrie, he'll play until he's 40-odd, so we gave him a new contract a year ago and that's that.'

He added:...

David James

Glen Johnson embraces David James at the final whistle after a dramatic climax to the Cup tie at Deepdale

David James is the hero once again as injury-time own goal gifts Pompey a scarcely-deserved place in the FA Cup quarter-finals

SMASH 'N' GRAB

QUARTER-FINAL

  MAN UTD 0   POMPEY 1

Pompey fans had tried not to broach the thought, but victory over Preston and a place in the last eight of the FA Cup meant they could resist the urge no longer. Could this be their year? Could this really be the moment their team seize upon their opportunity and go all they way in the grandest of all competitions?

All Harry Redknapp's men had to do was avoid champions Manchester United and Chelsea, and they would certainly fancy their chances of a securing a semi-final trip to Wembley at least. What fools we all were to hope. 'Number five Manchester United, will play number six Portsmouth.' In a moment, dreams of a day to remember at the home of football were shattered as they collided into the brick wall that was the prospect of a trip to Old Trafford. It was the draw nobody wanted, the draw which made every Pompey supporter sick to the stomach, the draw which made Redknapp launch his golf clubs in anger when the news was relayed to him by chief-executive Peter Storrie.

The feeling of destiny had been gathering pace. That now had been crushed under the weight of the most daunting of treks north to a theatre Pompey had not seen victory at for over half a century. A red machine lay in wait, a team who had been flexing its muscle in the Premier League on a seemingly inexorable charge towards its 17th top flight title.

United warmed up for Pompey by smashing in 12 goals in three domestic fixtures, and then seeing to Lyon in the Champions League for good measure. But Pompey were on an upwards curve themselves with three wins and a draw, before Redknapp's men came unstuck in a crucial European shootout at Everton. A 3-1 defeat at Goodison Park dealt the club's ambition of securing European football for the first time a massive blow. As if to acknowledge the point, Redknapp was at his prickliest in the bowels of Goodison Park in the wake of defeat. Hopes of a memorable finale to the campaign were fading fast, and the spectre of United on the horizon appeared likely to all but extinguish those ambitions.

As if further evidence of the mountain Pompey had to climb was needed, they had scored just four Premier League goals since their defeat at Old Trafford at the end of January. Jermain Defoe had scored three of them and he wasn't going to be adding to that total from the stands, as he sat the game out while cup tied. It was clear there was an Everest to ascend, and no one was giving Pompey a chance of coming through the expedition intact.

But those who wrote off this band of battlers hadn't factored the magic of the FA Cup into the equation. They hadn't taken into account the indomitable spirit of a team who don't know when to lie down and die. And they hadn't reckoned on Pompey delivering a performance which would go down as one of the greatest in their history.

SPORT

Muntari's so cool... I don't know how I kept out Carrick... Hawks' hopes hit... Festival Fever

THE DREAM IS ON

Contact the sports desk on (023) 9266 4488 | E-mail: sport@thenews.co.uk | www.portsmouth.co.uk

SPORT FOCUS

CHAMP OF THE DAY

POMPEY truly heroic display at Old Trafford to make the Cup semis. Now let's go all the way, boys.

CHUMP OF THE DAY

SIR ALEX FERGUSON Whinging after a defeat yet again and insisting Pompey were helped by the ref.

WHAT THEY SAID

'It's a worry. I want to see him back playing like he can'

Michael Vaughan on Steve Harmison's poor form.

YOUR VOTE

Today's question

Can Pompey go all the way and win the FA Cup?

Vote by logging on to www.portsmouth.co.uk and click Pompey Pages

59%

of the weekend's web poll said Kanu had been Pompey's best striker since their arrival in the Premier League.

21% believed Benjani had been the Blues' best forward in the top flight.

9% thought recent signing Jermain Defoe was the top goal-getter.

7% went for Teddy Sheringham.

2% chose Kanu.

2% said Lomana LuaLua

HARRY: I'M SO PROUD OF MY HEROES

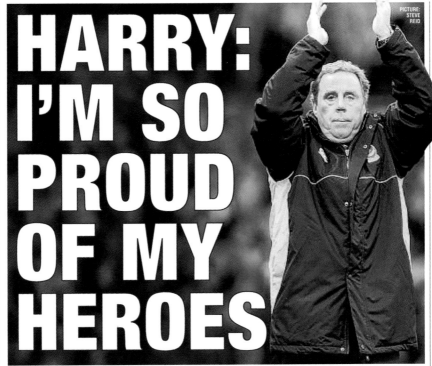

PICTURE: STEVE REID

by Jordan Cross
The News

Boss' delight at giving Pompey fans Wembley date and crack at the Cup

HARRY REDKNAPP today toasted one of Pompey's finest hours.

The Blues boss hailed Saturday's glorious FA Cup quarter-final victory over Manchester United as his best ever over the Red Devils.

Pompey fans were today in the midst of Cup fever with the club installed as odds-on favourites to win football's most famous domestic club competition.

They are now the only Premier League side left after Middlesbrough crashed out yesterday.

It means they will never have a better opportunity to lift the iconic trophy for the first time since 1939.

Redknapp has spoken of his personal delight at giving the people of Portsmouth their first trip to the home of English football for a major title since then.

And he lauded his heroes who stood firm with a supreme display, before

Sulley Muntari's 78th-minute penalty stunned the champions.

Now he feels they have a big opportunity to go all the way.

Redknapp said: 'It was a great day and a great performance.

'It's a great day for the club, the fans, the players and for me. I'm delighted.

'I've done it before against United but coming to Old Trafford and doing this is better.

'I've been ripped to bits here a lot of times before.

'We went back to the system we play with away from home and it worked.

'We had some big performances.

'I'm delighted the semi-finals are at Wembley now.

'If we weren't there I'd be

saying different, but now we're there I don't care!

'I'm going to look forward to leading the team out there. We'll have great support there and that's what it's all about. There are going to be all those supporters going to Wembley. It's going to be a great day for the people.

'I've never been to Wembley as a manager. Never.

'And I've never been to an FA Cup final. We're excited at the opportunity we have.'

An emotional Redknapp insisted the performance of his players on Saturday justified his decision to turn down a move to Newcastle in January.

He is now bidding for his first significant piece of silverware in football management after putting Pompey

in their first FA Cup semi-final since 1992.

Redknapp said: 'The strides we have made are amazing.

'I'm happy here and the people have treated me well.

'I had to win the fans over when I came back from Southampton.

'It wasn't easy but I hope I've done that now.

'I think I made the right decision in not going to Newcastle.

'It wouldn't have been right to bring all these players here, tell them what a brilliant club this is and go to Newcastle.

'I'm happy with that decision. My life is good.

'I have a good team here and with one or two additions we will be properly established. I have enthusiasm for what we are doing here.'

CUP CLASSIC
■ Pages 1-5, 19-25

Distin fires back after Ronaldo slams ref

by Steve Wilson
The News

SYLVAIN DISTIN has hit back at Cristiano Ronaldo's claims he didn't get the protection he deserved from the referee.

The skilful Manchester United star lashed out at referee Martin Atkinson in the wake of Pompey's remarkable 1-0 win at Old Trafford, revealing he was scared to play his natural game for fear of being badly injured.

Ronaldo said: 'Sometimes I say this is the best league in the world, but sometimes they don't protect the skilful players.

'After what happened to the Arsenal player Eduardo da Silva, I am scared to do my skills.

'The referee against Portsmouth

Sylvain Distin

was unbelievable. In the first five minutes, there were three fouls and he took no action and then he failed to give a penalty. It's difficult to play like this.

'It's a joke. So often, there were fouls and the referee did nothing.'

Distin, whose shoulder charge upended Ronaldo in the penalty area early in the contest, said: 'If every time you touch a player it is a penalty, then how do you defend?

'Football has to have some contact. I don't think he pushed the ball past me and I moved my body to stop his run.

'He pushed the ball, I followed the ball and it was shoulder against shoulder. If you can't tackle from behind, you can't do this, you can't do that, then you never defend.

'If he is coming towards me one against one, I am not going to move out of the way for him.

'I try to defend. All of the United fans thought it was a penalty, all of the Portsmouth fans and me will think it's not.

'For me, it was fair.'

FOR FULL REACTION TO TODAY'S FA CUP SEMI-FINAL DRAW, LOG ON TO www.portsmouth.co.uk

SPORT FOCUS

■ **CHAMP OF THE DAY**

STEVEN DAVIS
Midfielder netted Rangers' second goal as they defeated Werder Bremen 2-0 in the UEFA Cup.

■ **CHUMP OF THE DAY**

GILBERTO
Spurs debutant Gilberto's howler gifted Jefferson Farfan a goal in PSV's 1-0 win at White Hart Lane.

■ WHAT THEY SAID

'If I play them in the Champions League, I want to go there and kill them'

Jose Mourinho shows his desire to beat Chelsea when he returns to management.

■ YOUR VOTE

Today's question

How will Pompey fare against Manchester United tomorrow?

Vote by logging on to www.portsmouth.co.uk and click Pompey Pages

53%

in yesterday's web poll thought Harry Redknapp should revert back to a 4-5-1 formation, with Kanu up front, for tomorrow's FA Cup clash at Old Trafford.
■ 17% said Pompey should play a 4-4-2 with John Utaka partnering Milan Baros.
■ 14% believed Kanu should be dropped in favour of Baros playing the lone role.
■ 8% wanted a different shape.
■ 8% thought 4-4-2 was the best bet

Heart surgery leaves Pompey hit-man with nothing to fea...

KANU: RED DEVILS DO NOT SCARE ME AT ALL

by Steve Wilson
The News

KANU insisted Pompey could become FA Cup heroes in tomorrow's quarter-final encounter at Manchester United and revealed: I have no fear.

The gifted Nigerian striker thought his career was almost over before it began, when he was diagnosed with a faulty heart valve 12 years ago, just weeks after signing for Inter Milan.

But after surgery gave him a second chance, the Blues star knows all about fear – and insists Manchester United's galaxy of stars do not scare him.

Kanu said: 'Nothing scares me now. I have been through heart problems which is bigger than anything, so for me, I am relaxed.

'When you have gone through that, it gives you a perspective on life.

'The experience I went through with my operation makes you a stronger person – I have seen a lot.

'It takes away all the pressures on you.

'You realise there is a lot more to life than football.

'I don't play with fear.

'It doesn't matter who you are playing, you don't have to be afraid of anyone.'

His return to football was

Harry: Campbell will come good

HARRY REDKNAPP has backed Sol Campbell to bury the ghost of his Everton defensive nightmare.

The Pompey boss believes his captain will come good against Manchester United in the FA Cup.

Campbell *(right)* was at the centre of two of the mistakes which led to goals in Sunday's 3-1 loss at Goodison Park.

Redknapp acknowledged it was a rare off day for his back line.

But he believes a defence led by Campbell can silence Wayne Rooney, Cristiano Ronaldo and Co.

He said: 'Sylvain Distin and Sol Campbell have had great seasons.

'Glen Johnson has been in good form for us too.

'Sol has been here for two years and helped make us the top half team we've been for two years.

'He has been a massive player for us.'

an inspiration to many and the former Arsenal forward's influence on his Pompey team-mates will be a vital factor in the Old Trafford tie.

Kanu said: 'In Nigeria, when we play for the national team, we do not fear anybody – they are just men.

'That is the way football is supposed to be. If you go to Old Trafford afraid and expecting to lose 4-0, there is no need to travel.

'But this team does not fear anybody – even if we were playing against Brazil, Argentina or whoever. They are all just names.

'Of course Manchester United have quality players, but when they are on the field, they are on the field.

'There is no pressure.'

Kanu, who netted at Old Trafford in last season's fourth-round defeat, insists the big matches bring out the best in him – and he has fond memories of celebrating at Manchester United's home ground.

He recalled: 'When I was at Arsenal, we won the title there.

'I would say the big games bring the best out of me. You want to show the world you can play football and prove to everybody you are good.

'But the FA Cup means a lot to everyone in this country. I have been in England a long time and it means a lot to me now as well.

'We know how strong they are and how difficult it will be, but we are up for it.'

MANCHESTER UNITED 0 POMPEY 1 Harry Redknapp hailed his heroes after they delivered one of the greatest days in Pompey's history. Sulley Muntari scored the goal which sunk Premier League champions Manchester United in the FA Cup quarter-final at Old Trafford. That ensured Redknapp's battlers would be going to Wembley after making the last four of the famous old tournament. It was a day all Pompey fans will forever cherish as they picked up their first win on United's turf since 1957. And it meant the Blues would walk out at the home of English football for the first time since 1939. Redknapp lauded every one of his men for delivering a result that would go down in Fratton folklore.

floor. That gave United a sixth-minute free-kick which Paul Scholes headed wide from Nani's delivery. United had appeals for a penalty turned down after seven minutes when Ronaldo burst beyond Hreidarsson and was challenged by Sylvain Distin. It looked like a strong shoulder from the Frenchman but it was enough to have Ferguson screaming on the edge of his technical area as referee Martin Atkinson waved play on. Ferguson was still fuming as Joe Jordan berated Ronaldo for what he thought was a dive, leading to a tête-à-tête between the pair on the sidelines.

The 3,500 travelling Pompey fans had that sinking feeling after nine minutes when United were awarded a free-kick 25 yards out following a foul from Diarra on Scholes. The fear was it would be another blockbuster from Ronaldo but the Pompey wall did its job and

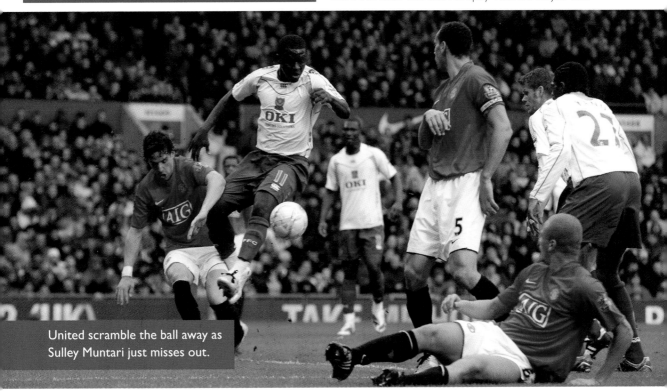

United scramble the ball away as Sulley Muntari just misses out.

It was a positive enough start from the Blues, with Lassana Diarra making some encouraging inroads into the home side's territory. His opening surge earned the Blues their first corner, but it was confidently dealt with by the United defence. Cristiano Ronaldo came in for some rough treatment from the visitors, with Diarra tackling the Portuguese midfielder and then Hermann Hreidarsson leaving him on the

blocked his drive. Pompey's first meaningful shot came from Niko Kranjcar after 16 minutes following another positive run but his 25-yard blast was gathered by Edwin van der Sar.

United had a glorious chance to snatch the lead after 19 minutes when Wayne Rooney and Carlos Tevez broke two on one against Sol Campbell. Tevez put the England international clean through with his pass, he rounded David James but Campbell's challenge saw the

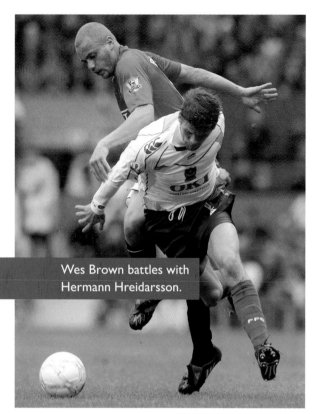

Wes Brown battles with Hermann Hreidarsson.

There was one significant half-time change for United as reserve keeper Tomasz Kuszczak replaced Edwin van der Sar. United started the second half the quicker, with Tevez burrowing away down the channel. There were signs of frustration creeping into the home side, though, when Ferdinand showed his anger after being penalised. But generally it was the home side who were on the front foot, although Pompey were standing firm.

The expected change in attack came from the visitors after 53 minutes when Milan Baros replaced Kanu. Pompey breathed a sigh of relief five minutes later when United looked certain to open the scoring. Nani's corner was met by Vidic's head, which James did well to keep out. The danger was not averted, though, with the ball loose in the box sparking a melee. Ronaldo eventually worked some space but his shot flew narrowly wide. Pompey fans were on their feet after 62 minutes when Baros got in behind the United defence. It looked like a golden chance was going to fall his way but referee Atkinson brought play back for a foul by the Czech striker on Hargreaves. Inevitably, United were starting to find spaces in the Pompey

ball ricochet to the Argentine. Tevez looked odds-on to score but his effort was cleared off the line by the covering Glen Johnson.

Rooney was the first United player in the book after 21 minutes for a foul on Kranjcar. He followed Pompey's Papa Bouba Diop, who had been cautioned for an earlier foul on Ronaldo. Pompey knew they could not afford to give away free kicks anywhere within range, but Diarra's foul on Tevez gave Ronaldo another opportunity to line up one of his howitzers. Luckily for Pompey, the wall again did its job and blocked his effort. United were in the ascendancy and pushing for the opener, but Campbell got his body in the way of Scholes' shot as he worked some space in the area. It looked like Pompey's best chance of a goal could come from a set piece. But Kranjcar had to do better than his wayward delivery following Brown's foul on Hreidarsson.

Pompey were enjoying periods of possession and some enterprising play led to Muntari finding some space, but his shot from distance was blocked by Hargreaves. Diop was the second Pompey player in the book 11 minutes before the break after Nani went to ground a little too easily after his challenge.

Muntari's penalty strike.

rearguard as a result of their pressure. Ronaldo looked as if he was going to beat James as space opened up for him inside the box, but the Portuguese superstar rolled his shot wide. United were really turning up the heat now, with Ronaldo's ball freeing Evra, but his cut-back was behind the on-rushing United players.

Ferguson made a double change with 22 minutes remaining as the Scot threw on Anderson and Michael Carrick in place of Rooney and Tevez. Some desperate

defending from Distin stopped a certain goal from Carrick two minutes later after he was played in by Ronaldo's back heel. It was incessant United pressure now, and Pompey had to rely on James to make a world-class stop and push Evra's 25-yard drive onto the post.

A moment of sheer drama turned the game on its head with 14 minutes remaining. Kranjcar broke clear from a ball over the top and played Baros free with a perfectly-timed pass. The Croat kept his composure and rounded Kuszczak but was hauled to the ground by the Polish keeper. Referee Atkinson had no hesitation in pointing to the spot and handing the United man a straight red card for a professional foul.

With no keeper on the bench, United were forced to put Ferdinand between the sticks. The tension had reached fever pitch but Muntari was the coolest man at Old Trafford as he stepped up and rifled a low drive to Ferdinand's left. That ensured the game's finale would be one of the most tense periods in Pompey's recent history.

Nails were being bitten in the away section and blood pressure was rising but Pompey held firm. Referee Atkinson found four minutes of stoppage time. But Pompey were playing down the clock well. And in the 95th minute, Atkinson blew the final whistle to ensure a famous win for Redknapp's battlers.

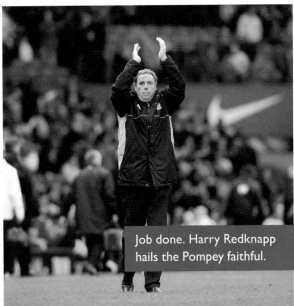

Job done. Harry Redknapp hails the Pompey faithful.

Lassana Diarra during another storming display.

Campbell clears from Wayne Rooney.

KEY MAN
SOL CAMPBELL

Pompey's skipper had to endure his fair share of flak going into this clash after an unsually below-par display against Everton the previous week. But what a way to silence the doubters. He embodied Pompey's gritty spirit with a rock-solid performance, keeping Ronaldo, Rooney and co at bay. It inspired a quite superb defensive outing from the Blues.

The turning point. Milan Baros goes down under the challenge from sub goalkeeper Tomasz Kuszczak.

Niko Kranjcar gets to grips with Ronaldo.

Campbell and Hermann Hreidarsson celebrate victory.

Pompey's Sylvain Distin clears off the line from Manchester United's Michael Carrick.

David James celebrates.

Pompey players show their delight after Muntari's penalty strike.

QUARTER-FINAL SUMMARY

This was already the year the underdog bit back in the FA Cup. But quarter-final weekend was to see them snarl more ferociously than ever. Pompey stunned the nation on the Saturday afternoon of March 8 with victory at Manchester United. Then that trend crazily continued later the same day, as Championship minnows Barnsley sent Chelsea's top-flight aristocrats spinning out of the competition. Kayode Odejayi was the Tykes' unlikely hero as he grabbed the only goal of the game at Oakwell. That sent the Yorkshire side into the semi-finals for the first time since 1912, when they went on to lift the trophy.

If that wasn't enough, Cardiff were to make it a hat-trick of upsets as they dumped Middlesbrough out. Boro, with such a big prize in sight, contrived to deliver a woeful display against Dave Jones' men. The Welshmen were in no mood to pass up such an opportunity, and seized a 2-0 win through goals from Peter Whittingham and Roger Johnson.

West Brom's 5-1 thumping of Bristol Rovers showed they had the firepower to be contenders as Ishmael Miller smashed in a hat-trick. James Morrison and Kevin Phillips got the others as the Baggies completed the last four line-up.

The News
Sports Mail

40p   **The weekly newspaper for fans and players alike**   Saturday, March 8, 2008

WE'RE GOING TO WEMBLEY

Muntari penalty enough for Pompey to cause Cup shock

MAN UTD	 0
POMPEY	 1

Sulley Muntari (pen) 78

Att: 75,463

READ JORDAN CROSS' BIG-MATCH VERDICT ■ PAGES 2-3

PORTSMOUTH
The News

WIN FAM... TICKETS TO BEAULIEU
PAGE 16

NEWSPAPER OF THE YEAR   Monday, March 10, 2008   40p   **FINAL**   www.portsmouth.co.uk

The big storm strikes
PAGE 9

WE'RE GOING TO WEMBLEY!

Semi-final ticket fever
PAGES 2&3

Blue Arm... goes barr...
PAGES 4&5

COMPAS...
Venture He...
WHERE EVE...
Contact: GREG...
Expansion means **we need gr...**
HELPING YOU TO SHAR...

The News

monday Sport
10.03.2008

FA CUP QUARTER-FINALS

Man Utd................0	Barnsley..............1	Middlesbrough........0	Bristol Rovers........1
POMPEY...............1	Chelsea...............0	Cardiff...................2	West Brom.............5

Sol Campbell salutes the away fans after the sensational win over Manchester United

Wembley-bound Pompey favourites for Cup after heroic win at Old Trafford
THE DREAM IS ON

SEMI-FINAL

WEST BROM 0 POMPEY 1

Que sera sera. We are going to Wembley. A heroic, gutsy, wonderful, beautiful victory at Manchester United paved the way for Pompey to make it into the last four of the FA Cup for the first time since 1992. Harry Redknapp had ended the barren run at Old Trafford, which had stretched back to October 19, 1957. And that meant Pompey were going to the home of English football for the first time in 66 years. The Blue Army were heading for the capital.

A defensive rearguard of stunning quality and Sulley Muntari's penalty had ended United's hopes of a treble in front of the watching nation. But what followed over the remainder of the weekend was to see an intoxicating sense of joy at slaying the champions replaced with the bizarre, but nonetheless very, very real, truth that Pompey were now favourites to lift the FA Cup.

Sensationally United's corpse was followed into the 2008 Cup graveyard by that of Chelsea's, who fell at Oakwell to Barnsley. The news was another adrenalin-inducing hit for supporters already high on the United victory. When Cardiff dismissed Middlesbrough's pathetic bid to make the semis 24 hours later, Pompey were left as the only Premier League team left in the competition.

Was this really happening? The sense of opportunity swept over the city in the ensuing days, as FA Cup fever took a firm grip. The news Pompey were to face

West Brom, the highest-placed Championship side of the three teams left in the competition, followed with Monday's semi-final draw. Then came the frenzied race to be at the game among supporters. Pompey were told they were to receive 'significantly more' than the 25,000 tickets allocated for last season's final. That was happily greeted, but it was clear the 32,500 eventually handed to the club would far from satisfy demand. Phone lines were jammed and then went into meltdown as punters jostled for the gold. Then came the camp-in at the last chance saloon, as followers queued overnight for the chance to grab the last 1,180 seats.

Things were buzzing on the pitch as well as off it, as Pompey picked up three wins from four to resurrect UEFA Cup ambitions. Birmingham, Aston Villa and Wigan were all defeated on a wave of Jermain Defoe's goals, with a single loss at Spurs coming along the way. Defoe's innate ability to find the back of the net delivered a record seven strikes in his first five home games, and eight across seven fixtures home and away.

But now it was time for a frenzy to take over Portsmouth. A sea of blue was to blanket the city as those with blood of that colour coursing through their veins showed allegiance to their team. Pompey were about to walk out beneath the infinite arch at the venue of legends, with their loyal infantry behind them. And they were to secure their date with destiny.

The News
FRIDAY, APRIL 4, 2008.

The News SPORT

Pompey v West Brom:
Semi-final special
– starts page 29

ON SALE NOW
WE'RE GOING TO WEMBLEY

For the BEST build-up to Pompey's FA Cup semi-final
Don't miss our We're Going To Wembley special, including

**Harry Redknapp
Sol Campbell
Wembley tour
Class of '92**

TIME TO SHOW THEM WE'RE ON THE UP

by Neil Allen
Chief sports writer

Campbell: Semi-final win will make world sit up and take note of Pompey

SOL CAMPBELL limbered up for Pompey's Wembley showdown and declared: It's time to make the world notice us.

The Blues head to Wembley in the FA Cup for the first time in 69 years tomorrow as they look to defeat West Brom.

For Campbell it represents an opportunity to not reach his sec

out on Europe by one point.

'Now we're having a great Cup run and it's worked out fantastic for us.

'We've played some good football and we've had a bit of luck on the way, which reach the Cup

Cup would the club, everyone the club, unt.

he media y down

than Pompey, but you have got to start somewhere and the Cup can be the place.

'Winning the FA Cup can really put this club on the map and get it noticed outside of this area.

'It can do so much good for the profile.

'It doesn't matter where you are, fans all love winning cups.

'But winning a cup with Portsmouth is going to mean a lot more than it would to the big four.

'We've got an opportunity, we have got to make sure we can capitalise and get to the final.'

Campbell has already lost three FA Cup semi-finals in a

glorious career at both domestic and international level.

And he believes it's important his team-mates focus on the job in hand against the Baggies tomorrow, rather than get distracted over what may happen in the future.

He added: 'It's the semi-final and people shouldn't get carried away and try to be a hero.

'It's all about getting through to the next round.

'I think it's going to be an exciting game, great for our fans, and I am definitely looking forward to it.

■ For the best reaction, reports and pictures from Pompey's semi-final at Wembley, don't miss the Sports Mail tomorrow and our 12-page special in Monday Sport.
BLUE DAY ■ Pages 1-6

Wembley D-Day for Pompey's injured duo

IT'S WEMBLEY D-Day for John Utaka and Hermann Hreidarsson.

The crocked duo were today set to discover their FA Cup semi-final fate having spent the week battling against injury.

Utaka has been troubled by a hamstring pull, while Hreidarsson's ankle has swollen after receiving three stitches to a gash in his Achilles.

Earlier in the week, the pair spent time in an oxygen chamber at the Royal Haslar Hospital in Gosport.

But both have still to return to training and have one last chance to prove their fitness ahead of tomorrow's West Brom clash.

And Harry Redknapp was set to make the final decision during today's final training session.

The pair have

John Utaka

responded well to treatment and shown an improvement as the week has gone by. But time is running out.

In the meantime, Lucien Aubey yesterday returned to training following a hamstring problem.

Should Hreidarsson fail to recover, the on-loan Frenchman will be on the bench, with Lauren set to deputise at left-back.

The replacement for Utaka is less clear, with the Nigerian the only genuine right-sided midfielder in Redknapp's squad.

The Blues boss may opt to employ either Milan Baros or David Nugent wide on the right in a 4-5-1 system.

Alternatively, he could hand Papa Bouba Diop an instant recall in a flat 4-4-2 formation – a role he has recently operated in.

Lassana Diarra will definitely start, though, alongside Sulley Muntari who is back from suspension.

Meanwhile, Kanu will line-up in attack.

PRICE: 40p

The News, 4 April 2008.

SEMI-FINAL SPECIAL

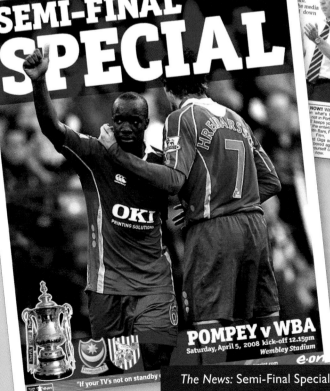

POMPEY v WBA
Saturday, April 5, 2008 kick-off 12.15pm
Wembley Stadium

e-on

The News: Semi-Final Special, 4 April 2008.

In order to show the city's support for Pompey at Wembley, *The News* organised a Blue Day on the eve of the cup semi-final. It gave locals the chance to show off their colours with a series of blue-themed events, while also raising money for the Tom Prince Cancer Trust, a fund set up to raise £1m in memory of one of the club's biggest fans.

PORTSMOUTH

The News

www.portsmouth.co.uk

NEWSPAPER OF THE YEAR

Friday, April 4, 2008

FINAL 40p

WE'RE GOING TO WEMBLEY!

IT'S A BLUE-TIFUL DAY

Inside: **16-page preview to Pompey's big match**

SEMI-FINAL **SPECIAL** INSIDE

WIN a family ticket to Paultons Park Plus: Music, movies and more

THE **GUIDE** INSIDE

WIN tickets to see Same Difference and meet them backstage PAGE 53

PORTSMOUTH FC FA CUP WEMBLEY STADIUM 2008

BLUE DAY: Thousands of fans show their true colours in an extraordinary show of support as Pompey head to Wembley

FULL STORY ■ PAGES 2,3,4,5,6&7

Pompey football club striker David Nugent (left) receives the £805 on behalf of the Tom Prince Cancer Trust, raised at Tesco Extra store, North Harbour, Portsmouth. The winner of the signed football competition, John Martin (35), of Hilsea, (right), with his prize.

Guildhall Square. Running a 'Kickpoint' and raising money for Blue Day was Richard Sexton.

Staff from the Co-op in Copnor Road lead by Kath Holloway (54), and in the gorilla suit, Stefan Rutherford (21), do their bit for *The News*' Blue Day appeal.

Cade Baker (13), Bradley Emmans (14) and John Long (12) of The Mary Rose School paint their faces for Blue Day.

Kanu tangles with Zoltan Gera.

POMPEY 1 WEST BROM 0 Pompey marched into the FA Cup final with a narrow victory over underdogs West Brom. Harry Redknapp's men were below par for much of the game – especially the first half – against their Championship opponents. But Kanu popped up in the 54th minute to give them a place in their first FA Cup final for 69 years.

The defining moment came when former Blues keeper Dean Kiely parried Milan Baros' shot and the veteran Nigerian was there to slot home from close range. Pompey could have even stretched their lead with both Baros and substitute David Nugent missing one-on-one opportunities late on. But as it was, Kanu's goal was enough to separate the sides and send the 33,000-strong Blue Army into delirium. It may not have been fluent, it may have been tense at times, but it didn't matter, Pompey were in the FA Cup final. The teams marched out of the tunnel amid a magnificent ticker-tape reception from Pompey fans. The Blues had the kick-off but it was to be their Championship opponents who adjusted to the occasion quicker. On four minutes, Kevin Phillips drove a shot narrowly over the bar following good work from Zoltan Gera.

Moments later it was the Hungarian winger who challenged on goal when he fired in a shot which James couldn't hold, and Sol Campbell pushed the ball clear with West Brom players closing in.

On eight minutes Pompey did threaten. Sulley Muntari's long ball from the left picked out the run of Milan Baros – but the striker couldn't collect and the ball skidded through harmlessly to Dean Kiely. James Morrison then found a way down Pompey's left to chip in a dangerous cross, which was met by the head of Phillips at the far post, although he failed to find a teammate in the box. The Blues supporters were doing most of the singing, yet sadly their side had still to raise their game on the pitch with the Baggies much the sharper in the early stages. Pompey's midfield were being harried every time the ball came near them, while Gera was looking a real threat down the right-hand side with his trickery.

It was clear Pompey had a real game on their hands. On 20 minutes, Baros thought he had carved a way through the visiting defence on goal, only to be adjudged to have fouled Paul Robinson in the process. It was proving tough going for the Blues but, importantly, it was still all square with plenty of gears to go through. Pompey launched a counter attack in which Diop put Baros through. But the on-loan striker took too many touches before being crowded out and the opportunity had gone. At the other end, Diop's slack clearance gifted possession to Gera but fortunately for Pompey his shot was wild. At least Pompey had a shot on target at the half-hour mark – their first of the game – with Kanu winning a free-kick which Muntari fired straight into the arms of Kiely.

Baros became the first player of the afternoon to be booked on 36 minutes after firing the ball into the crowd long after Howard Webb's whistle had blown. It summed up Pompey's frustrating start to the game and in particular the Czech Republic striker for who nothing was going right. David James almost provided a high-profile gaffe when he fumbled Glen Johnson's header back, allowing the ball to spring out of his arms. But he managed to retrieve it just in time with the onrushing Roman Bednar inches away. A piece of magic

from Kanu almost carved out another opportunity, but his clever lob fell into the path of Baros, whose outstretched foot could not connect with the ball. West Brom were still looking the better side, though, dominating possession and looking dangerous in attack. The growing frustration from Pompey fans echoed around the ground as half-time approached when Muntari was caught in possession with Pompey strongly placed to launch a counter-attack. The Ghana midfielder then fired in a left-foot rocket which flashed narrowly wide, although at least it was an attempt by a Pompey player. The fourth official indicated one minute of time added on, and Pompey were relieved to enter the interval still on level terms.

Harry Redknapp must have given Pompey a rollicking at half-time. And within nine minutes of the restart, they had broken the deadlock. Johnson's ball from the

Milan Baros sets up the winning goal.

David James makes a smart save.

right picked out Baros beautifully, who controlled it on his chest before firing a right-foot shot which Kiely parried. The keeper scooped the ball away from the onrushing Hreidarsson, but Kanu was on hand to coolly slot the ball into an unguarded net. Wembley exploded into life and suddenly the belief was there that Pompey had a foot in the Final. Moments later, Muntari surged into the box and pulled the ball back for Niko Kranjcar, yet his effort on the run screwed well wide. Already it was looking a completely different Pompey side from the one in the first half.

West Brom made two substitutions on the hour mark, Bednar and Morrison being replaced by Chris Brunt and Ishmael Miller, to try to turn things around. There were concerns when Diarra went down in the centre of the park and had to receive treatment, but he was fit to resume his midfield duties.

On 66 minutes, Baros missed a glorious opportunity to double Pompey's advantage with a dreadful miss. The former Liverpool striker was put through by Kranjcar with just Kiely to beat, yet opted to take several touches rather than shoot and the ball was bundled out for a corner. It was a golden opportunity spurned and in such a tight encounter could have proven expensive.

Pompey made their first substitution on 72 minutes with David Nugent replacing Baros. They were given a scare moments later when Hreidarsson slipped as he attempted to chase a long through ball putting Phillips clear, but James was swift off his line to claim the ball. But on 75 minutes West Brom came closest

to scoring yet again, with Robert Koren driving against the crossbar after an excellent run by Gera from the right. West Brom then made their final substitution, with Do-Heon Kim coming on for the impressive Gera. The game had developed into an absorbing contest and Muntari became the latest player to go close when his shot inside the box flashed just wide of the far post. Kranjcar then put Nugent clear through, but the Blues' substitute elected to hold up play and lay the ball back to Kanu rather than push through on goal.

On 81 minutes, Sean Davis came on to replace Kanu. Nugent missed a great opportunity to put the game beyond West Brom's reach when he fired straight at Kiely. At the other end, substitute Miller fired in a first-time shot which fizzed past the upright. The fourth official indicated three added minutes to ensure a nervous finish. Nugent could have sealed it on a Pompey break only to sky the ball following good work by Diarra. But it didn't matter, as Pompey reached the FA Cup final for the first time since 1939.

KEY MAN
KANU

Many said the striker was past his best. He may have not been able to cover much ground. But when you can make the ball stick to your feet like the Nigerian, you don't need to. It was a magnificent all-round striking display from Kanu. And he was in the right place at the right time to bag the winner and shatter his former club's FA Cup hopes.

Kanu, after scoring the winning goal.

Kanu tangles with Zoltan Gera.

Kanu scores the only goal of the game.

Celebrating Kanu's goal.

Milan Baros has a great chance to make it 2-0 but Dean Kiely saves at his feet.

Harry Redknapp in action on the touchline.

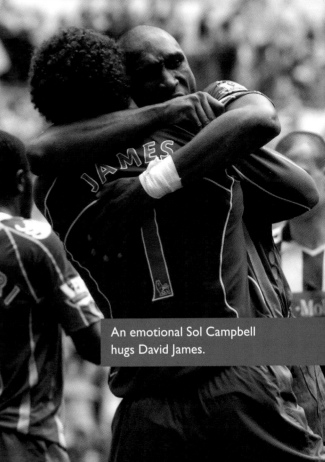

An emotional Sol Campbell hugs David James.

Sean Davis celebrates with Linvoy Primus.

Sean Davis, Kanu and Glen Johnston celebrate.

Kanu sends out a message.

Fans celebrate Kanu's goal.

Ryan Hudson (11) cheers Pompey on with the rest of the Portsmouth fans.

Pompey fans celebrate after the final whistle.

Joy as Pompey's fans celebrate Kanu's match-winning goal.

SEMI-FINAL SUMMARY

Joe Ledley was the man to break Barnsley hearts and earn a place in the Final for Cardiff. Ledley ensured it would be the unlikely Welshmen lying in wait for Harry Redknapp's men in English football's showpiece event, with the only goal in the other semi-final at Wembley. A sumptuous volley after nine minutes was the difference between the teams as Barnsley failed to deal with Tony Capaldi's long throw. It was perhaps apt that it was the player who had been with the Ninian Park side since he was eight who would put them in the final. In truth, it was never a classic match between two teams high on endeavour and determination, rather than outfits producing top-drawer football. Barnsley will look to the miss from Kayode Odejayi as their gilt-edged moment of opportunity. That came in the 66th minute as he went clean through from Brian Howard's lovely delivery, but somehow fired wide. It was a moment he and the rest of Simon Davey's side would rue as they failed to create a chance of similar magnitude. So it was left for Cardiff to hold on and let Men of Harlech ring around Wembley, as they secured their showdown with the boys from Fratton Park.

The News
Sports Mail

40p   The weekly newspaper for fans and players alike   **Saturday, April 5, 2008**

Nigerian striker tucks home winner to send Pompey through to the FA Cup final – and spark wild celebrations at Wembley

KAN-U BELIEVE IT

FA CUP SEMI-FINAL		
POMPEY		1
Kanu 54		
WEST BROM		0
	Att: 83,584	

PICTURE SPECIALS – PAGES 4, 5, 26, 27, 28

9 770963 388309   14

FAREHAM & GOSPORT

The News

Monday, April 7, 2008   portsmouth.co.uk   FINAL   40p

IN BLUE HEAVEN

BRING ON CARDIFF ■ 2&3   WEMBLEY WONDERLAND ■ 4&5   THE BIG POMPEY PARTY ■ 6&7   COMMENT ■ 8
MONDAY SPORT SPECIAL ■ 19,20,21,22,23,24,25,26,27,28,29&30

The News

monday
Sport

07.04.2008

Kanu pounces to send Pompey into the FA Cup final on a day of emotion at Wembley

Pompey skipper Sol Campbell embraces David James at the final whistle
PICTURE: WILL CADDY
(081357-6)

WE'RE THERE

FINAL

POMPEY 1 CARDIFF 0

 May 17, 2008

Now for the day of reckoning... Victory over a spirited West Brom had sparked joyous scenes at Wembley so violent on the eardrum, yet so pure in sound. The smiles on the faces of a city in the midst of a celebration said it all. Cars honked their horns as pubs, bars and homes rejoiced. People spilled on to the streets to revel in the moment. Portsmouth was a city exultant. Crikey, what was going to happen if Pompey actually went out and won the thing?

The biggest day in the club's modern history had been secured with semi-final success. May 17, 2008: The date for Harry Redknapp's men to seal their legacy. The moment for those players to deliver that performance loomed large on the horizon. First came the bid to continue rejuvenated hopes of finishing in the top five of the league. They had been re-ignited by victory at West Ham in the wake of success over the Baggies. Then came the 0-0 draw at home to Newcastle, which saw David James equal the club record for clean sheets, with his 22nd shutout of the season. But rekindled hopes of a Euro berth through the league were soon extinguished with the team's worst run of the season. Four straight defeats to end the campaign saw to that, as Manchester City, Blackburn, Middlesbrough and Fulham all turned over the Blues.

Pompey's form going into their first FA Cup final in 69 years was a concern. And worried furrows deepened as real concerns emerged over whether the immovable James would be fit for the game. A calf injury ended an unbroken run of 199 consecutive league appearances for Pompey's player of the year. Sol Campbell and John Utaka represented other worries from the treatment room. That news had gladdened Welsh hearts, with increasingly confident murmurs beginning to emerge from Cardiff and their fans.

Consciously or not, Redknapp clearly had his mind angled towards English football's showpiece occasion. It was the same for his players, as his assistant Tony Adams admitted in the wake of the Premier League closing defeat to Roy Hodgson's men. They were jostling for a place on the big stage though, with Pedro Mendes emerging as a realistic option to start after a composed final day appearance. Whether that would be in a 4-4-2 or 4-5-1 system was the big debate. Pompey had played their best stuff of the season employing the latter formation, although Redknapp's public statements said he was leaning to the former. Whether that was kidology or just Redknapp agonising over how to deliver his proudest moment in football remains open to debate.

The news from the club's Eastleigh base in the days leading to up to the final, was that Mendes was featuring in a five-man midfield when the team lined up in training. What was not in question was emotions were running high among supporters, as the moment to deliver edged closer. The word from inside the camp, however, indicated there were nothing but cool heads among the men charged with delivering the holy grail. A steely resolve and focus had kicked in. They were 90 minutes away from glory, one performance away from a victory which would echo in eternity. A worldwide audience of 500 million looked on. Pompey was expectant. Step forward Kanu. Long live the King.

IT'S THE FINAL COUNTDOWN!

The Blue Torch has run its journey..

..thousands are taking part in Blue2Day..

..passion for Pompey is everywhere to be seen..

..Harry says he wants to win it for the fans..

..and the Blue Army is ready for Wembley!

CUP FINAL BUILD-UP ■ **PAGES 3,8,9,10&11**   **COMMENT** ■ **PAGE 6**

INSIDE

The best Wembley preview:
16-page special on Pompey's big match

FA CUP FINAL SPECIAL
POMPEY v CARDIFF

PLUS

Wear Pompey's blue and claim a FREE doughnut

:: GREGGS

DETAILS ■ **PAGE 42**

PICTURES: ROBIN JONES

Harry calls on his men to go down in history by lifting Cup

From left: Kanu, Sol Campbell, Sulley Muntari and David James depart for their team hotel in Windsor yesterday

YOU CAN ALL BE LEGENDS

by Neil Allen
Chief sports writer

Diop and Mendes battle for a starting spot

Pedro Mendes

PAPA BOUBA DIOP is sweating on his place in Pompey's FA Cup final midfield.

The giant Senegal midfielder is under pressure for his spot in the engine room as Harry Redknapp mulls over his tactical options, with Pedro Mendes and Sean Davis both pushing hard for selection if the Blues boss plumps, as expected, for a 4-5-1 formation.

With David James and Sol Campbell both recovered from injury, Redknapp will announce the team at a briefing with the players tomorrow morning.

But barring any late injury scares, just one place is realistically up for grabs in the line-up.

Earlier this week, Redknapp hinted he is set to revert to the 4-5-1 formation that has served the team so well away from home, which would see Kanu start as the sole striker.

HARRY REDKNAPP challenged his players: Make yourselves legends.

Pompey stand on the brink of their first FA Cup final triumph for 69 years.

Tomorrow is Wembley D-day for Redknapp and his side as they bid to create club history when they take on Cardiff.

It has already been the best Blues season for more than half a century, with an eighth-placed finish in the Premier League.

Now they can add the famous old trophy to their remarkable achievements.

And Redknapp believes his players can achieve Pompey immortality with victory over the Bluebirds.

He said: 'It's the FA Cup final. If you can score in an FA Cup final you'll never be forgotten. But for all these lads, tomorrow is a chance to make themselves legends at this football club. They can write their names in history.

'What they achieve tomorrow can make them heroes with the fans.

'The players know what's at stake, they know what they are doing and they will be ready for Wembley to go out there and win the Cup.

'We have been preparing as best as we can and everything's gone well in the build-up.

'Now they've just got to go out and play. When they go out on to that pitch it's down to them completely. There's not a lot more I can do.

'These players have been absolutely brilliant this season – they have never let me down. They are good lads and that's why we will be there tomorrow.

'It's important not to get carried away by the occasion.

'They were nervous to begin with against West Brom and I am sure there will be nerves tomorrow – it's Wembley isn't it?

'It's been a great season and I am proud of all of them. They always rise to the occasion and we have a real chance of bringing this Cup back.'

The city will stand still tomorrow afternoon as they gather to cheer on their heroes.

At Wembley alone there will be around 25,000 roaring Pompey on against Cardiff, while Southsea Common will be packed with followers watching a specially-constructed big screen.

And for Redknapp, it epitomises just why it's the greatest domestic cup competition in the world.

He added: 'You think of all of the great fans at the game and back home – that's what it's all about.'

PRICE: 40p

9 770963 430350

Following the runaway success of Blue Day, which raised £50,000 for the Tom Prince Cancer Trust, *The News* followed it up with Blue2Day on the eve of the Cup final. Again the city turned blue as thousands of people showed their support for their team and for charity. Here Stamshaw School pupils do their bit by dressing in blue.

Leesland Junior School students Emily McNamara (11), Jake Grant (8), Jon Luke Grantham (11) and Billy Crow (11) help raise some money for the charity.

Southampton supporter Alison Wakefield dressed up in Pompey gear for the Blue2Day event.

Tom Hibberd and stepdaughter Victoria Moth at their café – Mumm's Café – in Southsea. They were supporting Blue2Day in memory of Victoria's mother and Tom's wife, Jan Hibberd, who died the year before.

The News

www.portsmouth.co.uk NEWSPAPER OF THE YEAR Saturday, May 17, 2008 FINAL 40p

POMPEY EXPECTS

First spelt out in flags that fluttered from heart oak warships on the eve of Trafalgar, it is a rallying cry that has resonated through the ages.

Nelson's immortal 'England Expects....' call-to-arms symbolises determination, valour – and victory.

And on this day of destiny, we invoke the spirit of the glorious challenge again. Because today, Pompey Expects....

In the hearts of the thousands of fans travelling to Wembley, of the legions gathering at pubs, clubs and homes around Portsmouth and of the countless more expatriate supporters around the nation and across the world, there burns a flame of immense hope and expectation.

Harry Redknapp and his team, who we have taken the liberty of transposing into William Overend's famous painting *The Hero of Trafalgar*, is our Nelson today – the leader of men who hold history in their hands. The hearts of countless thousands will be with them every step of the way as they strive for glory in this afternoon's FA Cup Final.

So Play Up Pompey – because today, Pompey Expects…

FULL STORY ■ PAGES 2,3, 46 ■ BLUE2DAY PAGES 4,5,17,18,31,32 ■ COMMENT, PAGE 6

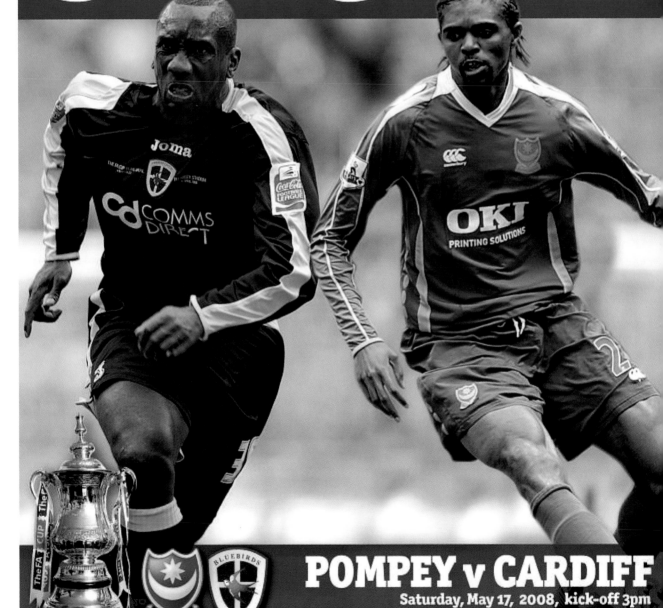

FA CUP FINAL SPECIAL

The News
FRIDAY, MAY 16, 2008

POMPEY v CARDIFF

Saturday, May 17, 2008, kick-off 3pm

Wembley Stadium

The Pompey starting line up for the final.

POMPEY 1 CARDIFF 0 The wait is over – the FA Cup is finally back in Pompey's hands. The man they call King Kanu will now forever be south-coast royalty after grabbing the only goal of the game to see off Cardiff. The Nigerian hit the winner on 37 minutes when he reacted to Peter Enckelman's fumble off John Utaka's deflected cross to stab home. That proved enough to bring the FA Cup back to Fratton Park for the first time since they won it in 1939. Harry Redknapp's heroes will now compete in Europe for the first time in the club's history, capping another outstanding season. Eighth position in the league and now the FA Cup is the culmination of yet more magic from that man Redknapp, who keeps on performing his heroics. Now Portsmouth will celebrate as they will never have done before. The FA Cup holders 2008: Portsmouth Football Club.

Pompey were given a tantalising glimpse of the atmosphere which awaited them when they made their way onto the pitch an hour before kick-off. Decked in their Jeff Banks suits, it was their first opportunity to survey the stage they were set to perform on. Many looked understandably pensive, while others, such as Sylvain Distin, maintained their focus by wearing earphones. The biggest cheer, though, was saved for Linvoy Primus, who wasn't even on the bench. Pompey's longest-serving player was greeted with chants of 'Linvoy, Linvoy' from the Blues faithful, prompting a wave and a big smile from the popular defender.

When Redknapp's side emerged in match kit some 20 minutes later, the Pompey flags were in full flight, dwarfing the efforts of the Cardiff contingent. There was a shock in store as well for Blues fans when the team was unveiled for the very first time. Pedro Mendes was given the nod ahead of Papa Bouba Diop in a surprise move by Redknapp. Earlier in the week, Pompey had trained with the 4-5-1 system, with Mendes in that same role. However, there were many eyebrows raised when the Portuguese midfielder was named in the side on Wembley day. Meanwhile, Kanu was chosen to lead the attack as the lone striker, with David Nugent and Milan Baros on the bench. Noe Pamarot was also there, his versatility and ability to operate at centre-half earning him the nod ahead of FA Cup final veteran Lauren.

There was amusement during the traditional rendition of *Abide With Me* when Katherine Jenkins' microphone stopped working during the second verse. Then there was the inevitable pantomime booing of both the

Wales and England national anthems from the opposing supporters. Redknapp's last act before the game was to hug his players individually and wish them all the best. It was a touching moment from a man on the brink of winning his first major honour in the game. Once the game kicked off the teams showed no signs of early nerves, with both keepers called into action during the opening exchanges. Pompey were certainly not affected by the same nerves which hampered their early progress against West Brom in the semi-final. However, there were several players who found it difficult to keep their feet on the skiddy surface, dampened by pre-match showers. Cardiff were also looking fearless and David James had to save well from Paul Parry in the 13th minute, while moments later Peter Whittingham's drive was deflected narrowly wide with James beaten. Early on it looked like this year's final was certainly going to be an entertaining affair. Kanu conjured up

the supporters unhappy with the lack of decisions they were winning. But the frustration turned to relief on 37 minutes when Utaka's cross from the right was collected and Peter Enckelman could only palm the ball out. There was Kanu two yards out this time to steer the ball home, giving Pompey the lead. It prompted the most bizarre goal celebration from the Nigerian, while Wembley exploded with Pompey's jubilation. It was the crucial breakthrough which largely, aside from Kanu's earlier miss, didn't look like happening.

Cardiff in particular were looking dangerous on the counter-attack – Parry's movement was a constant menace, with Campbell struggling to contain him. Meanwhile, wingers Niko Kranjcar and Utaka were struggling to get involved sufficiently to cause the Bluebirds damage. Deep into first-half stoppage time, Loovens thought he had pulled Cardiff level with a lofted half-volley from just inside the area, but referee

Sol Campbell and Hermann Hreidarsson challenge Paul Parry.

Kanu jumps over Cardiff's Glenn Loovens.

arguably one of the biggest FA Cup final misses when he somehow fired wide from three yards out. A fine move down the left between Hermann Hreidarsson and Sulley Muntari presented the Nigerian with the ball. And after cleverly losing his marker, Glenn Loovens, and dribbling around the keeper, he somehow contrived to smack the ball against the outside of the post with the goal at his mercy. You could hear the Pompey fans' frustration building, particularly with referee Mike Dean. Ironic cheers greeted his decision on 30 minutes to award a foul against Gavin Rae on Pedro Mendes,

Dean cut short the celebrations by adjudging the Dutchman had handled earlier. But Pompey went in at the break with that lead and the knowledge they were just 45 minutes away from lifting the FA Cup.

With Pompey in control of the scoreline, they opened the second half content to keep the ball. Undoubtedly, the Blues had the more talented players and they made full use of that with some patient play to starve Cardiff of possession. Kanu could have grabbed a second on 53 minutes when the outstanding Diarra surged down the left and pulled the ball back to the veteran striker,

A moment of drama! David James pushes the ball on to Glenn Loovens' arm before the Dutchman turns the ball into the Pompey net. Ref Mike Dean (right) blows the whistle for a handball.

whose effort was deflected wide. As for Cardiff, they were unable to keep possession of the ball, let alone launch an attempt at grabbing an equaliser. On 69 minutes, Utaka was replaced by David Nugent, with the winger appearing to be hobbling slightly, suggesting the substitution was forced. It meant Nugent was positioned on the right-hand side of Pompey's midfield, a role he only previously featured in occasionally for Preston.

Cardiff themselves brought on whiz-kid Aaron Ramsey and striker Steve Thompson in place of Whittingham and Hasselbaink. The move was designed to pep up Cardiff, although their fans appeared to have already lost heart

with the majority of their section sat in silence while Pompey continued to dominate. It was sensible stuff from Redknapp's troops, knowing they were in the driving seat with no need to chase the game. There was even an opportunity for Pompey fans to resurrect the Quashie chant in tribute to Joe Ledley, whose ambitious long-range effort was well wide.

Four minutes of extra time was indicated by the fourth official, prompting a nervy finish amid plenty of whistles from the Blues followers. But hold on they did to truly emotional scenes at Wembley for the club's greatest day for 69 years.

David James saves at the feet of Paul Parry.

KEY MAN
LASSANA DIARRA

On another level and far and away the best player at Wembley, Harry Redknapp pulled off a masterstroke by starting Pedro Mendes in midfield. That gave Diarra the freedom to express himself and show the world his fantastic ability. Cardiff could not stifle his control of the game, especially in the second half. Magnificent.

Kanu takes the ball around Peter
Enckelman only to hit the post.

Kanu sits on the ground in dismay
after missing an open goal.

Kanu lifts the ball over Enckelman to score the winning goal.

Kanu taps in the FA Cup winning goal after Cardiff's Peter Enckelman spills the ball.

Glen Johnson

David James

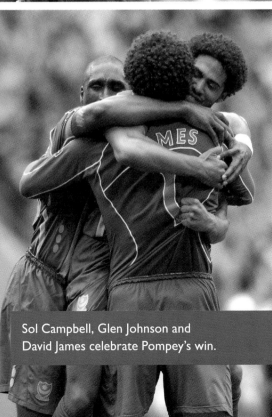

Sol Campbell, Glen Johnson and
David James celebrate Pompey's win.

Kanu celebrates his man-of-the-
match performance with Sylvain
Distin at Wembley.

Niko Kranjcar, Sylvain Distin and Noe Pamarot celebrate Portsmouth's win.

Pre-match: *Abide With Me* was a bit of a mess with microphones failing, but nobody seems too bothered. Pompey are in party mood and the players are in the tunnel. Harry Redknapp was nearly in tears as he led Pompey out for their biggest match in recent history. There were boos for both national anthems, unsurprisingly perhaps, but a little sad nonetheless – it felt more like England v Wales than Pompey v Cardiff. Harry Redknapp was bubbling with emotion, though, and hugged each of his players before the game. Pompey walked out all in blue with Cardiff in black. Pompey kicked off, attacking the Cardiff fans in the East Stand.

01: A quick foul on Diarra let Muntari have a pop from 30 yards but the shot was deflected and Enckelman saved.

02: James had to put a long ball out for a throw. Pompey cleared the danger.

06: Another long throw from Capaldi and Mendes headed out for a corner.

11: Pompey tried to be methodical in their play and there were a few snappy challenges – from both sides.

13: Kranjcar was at the heart of most of Pompey's best play and a probing run ended when he knocked the ball just too far.

13: A big chance for Cardiff – Paul Parry broke inside of Campbell from a Ledley pass but James made a fine block.

14: Cardiff ask the questions. Whittingham's shot is deflected just wide with James beaten.

15: Pompey get on the front foot. A Muntari free-kick is punched by Enckelman, but only on to Distin, who couldn't react to direct his header into the open net.

19: Quality play from Diarra left two Cardiff players for dead but he couldn't pick out Utaka's run.

20: Campbell headed a Cardiff free-kick behind for a corner and James eventually gathered with confidence.

21: Utaka fell over – for the third time! It was like he'd left his studs at home.

23: It was one of the biggest misses in Cup Final history – Kanu produced real class to take Loovens out of the game with one touch, and round Enckelman with the next from a Muntari cross, but somehow he rolled the ball against the post and wide.

24: Cardiff get back into it. Johnson fouled Ledley and Pompey just avoided danger from a set piece.

25: There was no let-up in the action as Cardiff won a corner, which Whittingham drifted out. It was high-octane stuff in football's showpiece event.

27: A Whittingham free-kick was headed over by Johnson.

29: Parry began to cause real problems with his movement, but James was quick off the line to deny him from a through ball.

33: Hreidarsson advanced and found Kanu. He cut inside but miscued his shot from the edge of the box.

34: Pompey's pressure saw Johnson maraud forward and Enckelman punch clear his cross. Then Mendes hit one from 30 yards – but the Cardiff keeper gathers.

37: **GOAL!** Pompey take the lead! Utaka did a number on Capaldi down the right and whipped in a lovely little cross which Enckelman could only half-block, and there was King Kanu to nip the ball in from a couple of yards. Pompey's Blue Army went crazy and blew the roof off Wembley!

39: A brilliant block tackle from Campbell denied Hasselbaink.

40: Hearts were in the mouth as Cardiff broke three on two. Parry cut in and crossed, but McNaughton couldn't control his shot with the goal gaping.

44: 'Sol goes up to lift the FA Cup, Wembley! Wembley!' roared the Pompey faithful. A little prematurely perhaps, but the 25,000-strong travelling army was buzzing.

45: Hreidarsson goes into the book for what appeared to be dissent.

45: Cardiff have a goal disallowed after a Ledley corner. James flapped and Distin tried to clear, but Loovens blocked with his arm before lifting a shot into the net. Mike Dean was on the spot and awarded a foul.
Half-time: Pompey 1-0 Cardiff

46: Cardiff restarted the game.

48: Mendes really justified his inclusion with some calm passing to get Pompey started.

50: Utaka crunched Ledley and was given a talking to by ref Dean.

51: Cardiff fans were cheering as Johnson met Whittingham's free-kick at the back post, but it was only into the side-netting.

53: Pompey have a great chance for a second. Diarra marauded forward again and exchanged passes with Kranjcar, who returned the ball with a lovely flick before cutting back to Kanu. The Nigerian had time, but scuffed his shot and Loovens put his chest in the way to block. It was a big opportunity.

55: Kranjcar was booked for a foul which stopped Whittingham breaking clear for a decent attack.

56: Muntari thundered a chance just over from 30 yards.

61: Ramsey replaced Whittingham for Cardiff.

65: The pace slowed for the first time in the match, but there was a feeling around the ground that there was more drama ahead.

68: Pompey were upping the pressure through Diarra. He found Kranjcar, but the Croat slipped.

69: And then came 'the Noog'. Utaka was replaced by David Nugent.

70: Cardif made changes too with Hasselbaink replaced by Steve Thompson.

71: Nugent broke clear and fired a shot from a tight angle which Enckelman tipped over.

73: Ledley fired well over with a speculative effort from distance.

74: The noise level dropped from the Pompey fans for the first time in the game – perhaps they sensed the Cup was moving closer and closer as each minute passed.

75: Johnson continued to threaten from set-pieces, but headed a Cardiff corner over.

78: Diop replaced Mendes, who was given a standing ovation.

79: A Thompson cross is put behind for a corner by Distin, and it is headed over by Loovens.

81: Johnson killed Cardiff pressure by seeing the ball over the dead ball line.

83: Pompey broke through Kranjcar who fed Kanu, but McNaughton dealt with his threat.

85: What a run from Distin! The defender charged 45 yards before just failing to get his shot off.

86: Baros is the final substitution for Pompey, who replaced Kanu. Sinclair came on for Rae.

88: Cardiff powered forward through McNaughton and Ramsey, but Pompey somehow got bodies in the way.

89: Kranjcar freed Baros, who won a corner which Cardiff dealt with.

90: Four minutes of stoppage time.

90: James collected a long punt.

90: Diarra was booked for a foul on Loovens. Cardiff charged forward but Campbell put it behind for a corner, which James eventually gathered.

Full-time: **Pompey 1-0 Cardiff…Pompey are FA Cup winners!**

Kanu gets round Peter Enckelman to score.

The News

monday

Sport NE

19.05.2008

TheFA CUP e·on

Pompey celebrate winning the
FA Cup after beating Cardiff
1-0 in the final at Wembley
PICTURE: STEVE REID (082214-921)

Glory for Pompey: Kanu's Wembley

CUP H

The News

40p

Sports Mail

The weekly newspaper for fans and players alike

Saturday, May 17, 2008

POMPEY WIN THE CUP!

**Harry and Campbell lift the silverware after Kanu's
winner seals glory for the Blues heroes at Wembley**

REPORTS AND PICTURES ■ PAGES 2&3, 4&5, 6&7, 8&9, 10&11, 28

POMPEY	1
Kanu 37	
CARDIFF	0

NR: 80,874

Manager Harry Redknapp with the FA Cup.

Sol Campbell lifts the FA Cup.

Kanu with the FA Cup.

Sol Campbell with David James and Sylvain Distin.

The club celebrate with the Cup and lots of champagne.

When Sol Went Up to Lift the FA Cup

CUP FINAL STATS

TACKLES SUCCESS:
Pompey 78.9%
Cardiff 67.6%

POSSESSION:
Pompey 49%
Cardiff 51%

TERRITORIAL ADVANTAGE:
Pompey 49.4%
Cardiff 50.6%

SHOTS ON TARGET:
Pompey 5
Cardiff 3

PASSING SUCCESS:
Pompey 80.6%
Cardiff 68.1%

SHOTS OFF TARGET:
Pompey 6
Cardiff 6

YELLOW CARDS:
Pompey 3
Cardiff 0

CORNERS:
Pompey 6
Cardiff 7

RED CARDS:
Pompey 0
Cardiff 0

FOULS:
Pompey 23
Cardiff 9

TACKLES:
Pompey 19
Cardiff 34

OFFSIDES:
Pompey 4
Cardiff 2

BLOCKED SHOTS:
Pompey 1
Cardiff 3

TOMORROW: HUNDREDS OF POMPEY FANS IN OUR 16-PAGE PICTURE SPECIAL

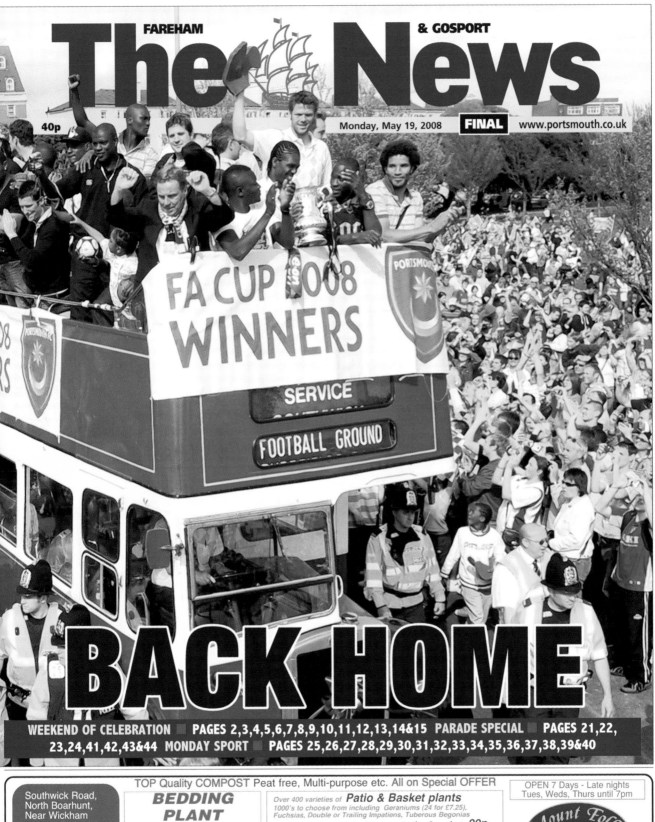

FAREHAM The News & GOSPORT

40p

Monday, May 19, 2008 **FINAL** www.portsmouth.co.uk

FA CUP 2008 WINNERS

SERVICE

FOOTBALL GROUND

PORTSMOUTH

BACK HOME

WEEKEND OF CELEBRATION ■ **PAGES 2,3,4,5,6,7,8,9,10,11,12,13,14&15 PARADE SPECIAL** ■ **PAGES 21,22, 23,24,41,42,43&44 MONDAY SPORT** ■ **PAGES 25,26,27,28,29,30,31,32,33,34,35,36,37,38,39&40**

The view from the corner of Kings Road and Landport Terrace of the Pompey parade.

The Pompey victory parade travelled from Fratton Bridge out to Southsea Common, and was cheered on all the way.

The victors wave to the adoring Pompey fans.

Fans went to great lengths to catch a glimpse of the Pompey parade bus.

Fans greet the victory parade on Southsea Common.

The Pompey team bus works its way through a sea of fans.

Hermann Hreidarsson leading the celebrations on stage.

Harry Redknapp leads the singing of the Pompey Chimes.

Sacha Gaydamak holds the Cup aloft.

Thousands turned out to celebrate Pompey's victory.

The parade arrives at the corner of Kings Road and Landport Terrace.

CONCLUSION

Their place in the pantheon of greats has been assured.

The heroes of 2008 will stand alongside the legends of 1939. Pompey are FA Cup champions.

Joyous visions from the road to success will endure in the memory of every Blues fan. They have shown resolve to stand firm in bleak times, and now stand triumphant. A journey that no one could have predicted has delivered a victory to make every follower of the star and crescent burn with pride. Next comes the march on Europe.

The glory of lifting the grandest of club knockout trophies is reward enough for Pompey fans. But it doesn't stop there. Now for Paris, Hamburg, Lisbon, Berlin, Seville, Athens and the rest. Football on some of the grandest stages across the continent has been secured for the first time in the club's history. Another voyage of discovery lies in wait.

Nobody knows where the next chapter will take us. But not knowing when the twist, turn or bump is coming is what makes following this club such a unique experience. Where Pompey go, drama follows. The two are irreversibly entwined. But we should never take these halcyon days for granted. We all remember it wasn't too long ago the club we all care for was on life support in critical condition.

So revel in the afterglow of a triumph that will endure forever. Savour every last drop of the sweetest of successes ever tasted. Remember every mile clocked up along the way, every joke, laugh and moment of camaraderie. Then get ready for the next stage of the white-knuckle, adrenalin-filled rollercoaster ride that is Portsmouth Football Club.

Fasten your seatbelts, because we're all going on a European tour!

FAN
PAGES

Danny Abat
Frank Abbott
Mick Abrams
Jan & Cath Absolom
Colin Adams
Margaret Adams
Nigel Adams
Joe Addyman
Ray Adlam
Andy Aggar
Nick Aldridge
Alex Alexander
Neil Alford
Alfie Allen
Jenny Allen
Mark Allen
Oscar Allen
Paul Allen, Gosport
Peggy Allen
Tom Allman
Bradley Amor
Ben Anderson
Nicola Andrews
Terry Andrews
James Anderson Jnr
Macaulay Antell
Lewis Archer
Paul Argyle
Martin And Matthew Arnell
Michelle And Mark Arnell
Bradley Arnott
Ryan Arnott
Tracey Arter
Andrew R Atkinson
Richard Attrill
William Austin
Michael Averre
Christopher Manuel Avery
Kelly Avery
Kerry Aylmer
Brett Ayton
Thomas Giles Babb
Michael Babbage
Andrew Bailey
Stephen John Bailey
Des Baines
Steven Baker
Ted Baker
John A Baldock
Bradley Baldwin
Darren Ballard
Rob Banfield
Iain Graeme Bryan Banks
Roger Banks
Thomas Banks
James Banting
Kevin Banting
Matt And Sally Barber
Stephen Barclay
Christopher John Bareford
Tristan Peter Bareford
Ken Bargery

Alex Barnard
Bryn Robert Barnard
Gareth James Barnard
Matthew Barnard
Bradley Barnes
Mike Barnes
Mr J F W Barnes
Teresa M Barnes
Tony Barnes
Laurence Barnett
Adam Barrett
Mike Barter
Billy Bartholomew
Harry Bartholomew
Andy Bartlett
Catrin Bartlett
David Bartlett
Dennis Bartlett
Mark Bartlett
Paul Bartlett
Harry Jake Barton
James Barton
Steve Barton
Philip Basford
Phil Beal
Graham Beale
Mark Beavis
Richard Beavis
Valerie Beavis
Harry Bedford
Graeme Bell
Jim Bellinger
Carol Benet
Paul Benet
Alan Bennet
David W Bennett
Michael Bennett
Iain Bennett-Hobbs
David Best
Jeremy Betterton
Michael Betts
Paul Biginton
Simon Billingsley
George Bird (1936-1987)
John Bird
Michael Bird
Philip Bird
Tony Bird
Andrew Bishop
Harry Adam Bishop
Trevor Bishop
Jack Blackburn
Joan Blackman
Peter Blades
Sarah Blake
Jim Blanden
Calvin Blandford
Michael Blitz
Russell Blitz
David Boggust
Matthew David Boltwood
John Bond

Michael John Bond
Jason Bonner
David Bonner-Smith
Steve Bonney
Tom Borrow
Graeme Bosbery
Kev Boudier
Mark Bowen
Paul David Bowen
David Bowers
Kim Bowers
James Spike Boxall
Paul Boynton
Brydon Brassett
Jack Brassett
Eric Brett
Sally Brett
Val Brewerton
Joe Briant
Brian Briggs
Colin Britton
Lee Britton
Liam Britton
Jonathan Broderick
Thomas & Annabelle Brooker
Colin Brooks
Hans, Oli & Jess Brooks
Mike Brooks
Olivia & Jacob Brooks
Robin Brooks
Andy Brown
Bernard Anthony Brown
David Brown
George Brown
Liam Brown
Lloyd Brown
Russell M Brown
Scott R. G. Brown
David Brumwell
Andy Bryant
Arnold Bryant
Ashley Bryant
Roger Bryant
Russell Buchanan
Steve Bucksey
Paul Buckland
David Buckley
Carl Bucksey
Albert Charles Bulbeck
Jen Burbridge
David R Burch
Robbie Burchell
Daniel Burford
Terry Burgess
Steve Burghard
John Burnett
Bruce Burr-Lonnon
Christopher Burt
Keith Burton
Mark Burton
Ben Busby
Anthony Bushnell

Roy Butchart
Jason Butcher
Steve Byrne
Kye Cadman
John Caisley
Christopher Callaway
Jim Campbell
Scott Campbell (
Pompeydownunder)
Darren Cane
Percy Cannon
Brian Henry Card
Andy Carlisle
Robert Carlisle Jnr
Steve Carlisle
Dave Carr
Harry Michael Carroll
Michael Andrew Carroll
Samuel Carter
Keith Casey
David Cawdeary
Gerry Cawdeary
Annie Chamberlain
Guy Chamberlain
Steve & Laura Chamberlain
Darren Chambers
Mark Ian Chambers
Tim Chandler
Nick Chant
Carl E Chapman
Malcolm John Chapman
Peter Cheesman
Bryan Cherry
Laurence Cheyne
Fraser Childs
Robert Childs
Ronald Chivers
Patrick Chubb
Dave Churcher
Max Churcher
Paul Churcher
Robert Churcher
Karen Churchill
Colin Clark
Derek J Clark
Neil J Clark
Sharon Christina Clark
Garry Clarke
Graham Clark
Gregg Clarke
Harry Alan Reggie Clarke Born
06.06.08
Jane Clark
Brian Clay
Antony Clements
Bradley Clements
Dean Clements
Louis Clements
Matthew Clements
Michael Clements
Vicky Clements
Victoria Clements

Daniel Clewes
Alan Clifton
Gavin Clifton
Michael Clifton
Craig Coan
Paul Coates
Sasha Cochrane
Oliver Cocking
Dennis Cole
Paul Cole
Jake Coleborn
Gordon Coleborn
Ryan Coleshill
Rob Collier
Tyrone Collier
Cole Collins
Mick Collins
George Collyer
Paul Collyer
Steven Colwell
Grant & Claire Combes
Paul & Dianne Comparini
James Conway
Brian J Cook
Gary & Darren Cook
Titch Cook
Bradley Coombes
Elliott Coombes
David 'Rolfie' Coombs
Keith Coombs-Goodfellow
Roy Coombs-Goodfellow
Brett Cooper
Brian Mark Cooper
Don Cooper
Gerald Cooper
John Cooper
Matthew Cooper
Michael Cooper
Mr John William Cooper
Neil Cooper - Florida
Kevin Corney
David Corps
Neal Costen
Antony Cotton
Callum Courage
Michael Courage
Kev Courtney
Dave Cousins
Billy Cox
Paul Fred Cox
Alan Crabb
Lynsey Craggs
Rob Craig
A R M Cripps
Alan J Cripps
Graham & Ryan Cripps
Sarah Crockett
Vicky Crockford
Anthony Cronin
Liane Crosby
David Cross
Mike Cross

Steve Cross
Steve Cross Jnr
Tony Cross
Wayne Cross
Colin Croucher
Sam Croucher
Spencer Croucher
Kev Croughan
Leslie Crowhurst
Danny & Nick Crown
Mandy & Tom Cruden
Mick Cubitt
Lee Culshaw
Glyn-Owen Cummings
John Curtin
Bill Curtis
Keith R Curtis
Laurie K Curtis
Kathryn Cuthbert
Carl Davey
Sue Davidson-Purrington
Joseph And Iaan Davies
Mike Davies
Nathan Davies
Roger, Harry & Charlie Davies
Ron Davies
Bryan Davis
Peter Davis, Karen Davis And
Harry Davis
Shaun Davis
Stephen Davis
Dave Dawkins
Derrick Day
Micky 'Snapper' Day
Brian Daysh
Ian Daysh
Lee Daysh
John Dean
Thomas Dean
Zack Dearie
Gary Dean
Simon & Sian Deary
Sym And Raz Deary
Ross Deck
David Denham
Tony Denning
Martin Dennison
Rob Dennison
Tony Denyer
Andy Derrick
Colin Dey
Gavin Dey
Jasper Di Marco
Diana, Nicola & Steve
Rog & Sam Dicken
Ian Dickie
Roy & Shirley Dickie
Jonathan Didymus
Mark Didymus
Zach Diment
Simon Dines
Adam Disney

Edward Ditchburn
Eddie Dix
Steve Dixon
Zach Dixon
Oliver Dockerill
Elaine Dore
Chris Doust
Kevin Doust
Steve Dowdell
Steve Drage
Frank Drain
Jonathan Andrew Dray
Christopher Draycott
Malcolm Drew & Robert Boswell
Peter & Mary Drew
Marcus Dudman
Peter Dudman
Mark Dugan
Mr Jaime Duggan
Paula Duggan
Steve Duke
Julie Dunbar
James Duncan
Michael Duncan
Nathan & Sally Duncan
David Lewis Dunn
Jerry Dunn
Karen Dunsford
Mark Dunsford
Brian Dutton
David Dyer
Callum Eade
John Eames
Mat Eastman
Ann Eaton
Ben Eaton
Gareth Eddington
Mick Eddy
Gordon & Linda Ede
Neil Edgar
Gary Edney
Martin Edney
Richard Edney
Arran Edwards
Colin Edwards
Julie Edwards
Liam D Edwards
Peter Edwards
Rod Elkington
Michael Elliott
Simon Elliott
Sue Elliott
Neil Elsegood
Jeremy George Elwall
Clive Embling
David Emery
Michael Emery
Neil Emery
Roger Emptage
Stan Emptage
David T Evans

Mike Evans
Ashley Eyers
Clare Farnell
John Farnell
Michael Farr
John Farrand
Laura Farrand
Dave C Fay
Gary Fearon
Jake Featherstone
Chris Fehrenbach
John Fehrenbach
Ron Fehrenbach
Tim Fehrenbach
John Fellows
Andy Fenner
Ross Ferguson
Deb Fernee
Donovan Ferns
Mark Ferre
Sarah Ferre
Keith Fiander
Ant Figgins
Graham Figgins
Chris Filmer
Chris Fisher
Paul Fisher
Chris & Anne Fleming
Claire Fleming
Dall Fletcher
Kenneth Fok (Vancouver)
Andrew J Ford
Peter Forsyth
Brian Foster
Terry & Sarah Fowler
George Francis
Andrew Fraser
Andrew Frearson
Mr A Freer
Dave French
Paul French
Daniel Friend
Craig Fryer
Kelly Fryer
Norman Fryer
Anthony Gaffney
Bob Gale
Charlie Gale
Ted Gant
Paul Edward Gardner
Ian Gates
Lee Gatfield
Steve George
Dennis Gerring
David Gershkoff
Lynda & Chris Gibbs
Tom Gilbert
Jessica Gilby
Karen Gillespie
Graham Gillians
Paul James Gillingham
Dave Glass

Christopher Glanville
Bradley Goble
Darryl Goble
Paul Goble
Dave Godding
Tim Godfray
Stephen Godfrey
Ben Godliman
Richard S Goldstone
Adam Goodacre
Christopher Goodall
John Goodall
Dave Gordon
Chris Gorman
David Goswell
Dave Gould (Wavey)
Jack Gould
Paul David Gould
Simon Gould
Joseph & Marcus Gowers
Bill Graham
Gary Graham
Len Graham
Peter Graham
Richard Graham - I Was There
Roger Graham
Neal Grainger
Kevin Grant
Robin Grant
George Gray
Neil Gray
Richard Greaney
Daddy J Green
Duncan Green
Emily Green
Michael James Green
Scott Green
Steve Green
Matthew Greenfield
Mike Greensmith
Gregogs
Ali Gregory
Daniel Gregory
Melvyn Gregory
Paul Gregory
Ian Grey
Evie And Maisie Grice
Mark Grice
Andrew Griffin
David Griffin
Peter Griffin
David & Sam Griffiths
David Griffiths
Ken Griffiths
Owen Griffiths
Mark Grist
Gez Groom
Shane Wield Grout
David Groves
Grumps
Colin Gutteridge
Chris Guyatt

Finley Hadaway
Mike Hadley
Rex Haines
Kenny Hall
Philip Hall
Tony Hall
Steve And Toby Hallett
Josh Halsey
Nick Hambleton
Michael Hamlet
Kevin Hammal
John Hammond
Jordan And Ellis Hampton
Bob Hanbry
John Hancock
Mark Hancock
Martin Hancock
Gary Hankers
Derek Hannam
Darren Hanvey
Ethan Hanvey
Mr A Hardy
Jim Harfield
Kevin Harfield
Phyllis Harfield
Dave Harkness
Barry Harmer
Jack Harpur
John Harmer
Michael Harper
Robert Harper
Rory Harper
Ryan Harpur
Alex Harris
Carole Harris, Aus
Cyril Harris
David Harris
David Harris
Gregory Harris
Jo Harris
Josh Harris
Kay Harris
Keith Harris
Lee Harris
Liam Harris
Malcolm Harris
Nicholas Evan Harris
Paul Harris
Susan Harris
Roy Harrison
Mr N E Hart
Ben Hartley
Nick Hartley
Len Harton
Lew Harton
Luke & Mark Harvey
Andy & Rufus Harwood
Andrew Hasker
Paul & Alison Hatch
Peter Hatch
Ron Hatton
Jason Hawen

Kev Hawker
Clive Hawkins
Ken Hawkins
Nick Hawkins
William Philip Haydon
Derek Hayes, Lisa Hayes, Jodie
Hayes, Billy Hayes
Harry Haynes
Luke Haynes
Paul Haynes
Mr Guy Haywood
Christine Healy
John Heap
Paul Hearn
William Hearn
Barry Heath
Oakland Louis Heath
Heather & Julie
Eddie Helbert
John Hemming
Colin Hempsey
Michael Henning
Andy Heron
Dale Herridge
Jonathan Hewett
Sean Hewitt
The Higgins Family (Fareham)
Paul Higgs
Brian Hill
George Ieuan Hill
Matthew David Hill
Mike L Hill
Matt Hinks
Philip Hinks
Toby, Andrew, Richard And
Debbie Hinton
Sean Mark Hoar
Marcus Aaron Hoare
Michael Hoare
Barry John Hobbs
Ian Hobbs
Lynda Diane Hobbs
Peter Hobbs
Trev Hobbs
Darren Mark Holden Rip
Graham Holding
Emma Holloway
Mark Holman
Ann Holmes
Bill Hooper
Chris Hooper
John Hooper
Derek 'Choppo' Hopkins
Jeff Horler
Bryan Horn
Paul Houghton
Jamie Hounsome
Rupert Howell
Dennis Hoy
Matt Hoy
Christopher Hughes
Dan Hughes

Peter Hulbert
Stephen Hulbert
Chris Clark Humphries
Dave Hunn
Andy Hunt
Geoff Hunt
Jayne & Malcolm Hunt
Liam Hunt
Paul Hunt
Tom Hunt
Janet And John Hunter
Peter Hunt
Stephen John Paul Hunter
Dave Huson
Jacob Hussey
Martin Hutchinson
Paul Hutchinson
Lee Hutton
Ivor George Inseal
Kevin Ivatt
Ian Jacks
Andrew Jackson
Bob Jacobs
Robert Jacobs
John James
Paul Jamieson
Thomas Jamieson
Aston Jays
Russell Jays
Jeff
Peter Jeffers
Nathan Jeffery
J M Jeffery
Derek Jennings
Rob Jerram
Andrew Johnson
Bradley William Shankly
Johnson
Geoff Johnson
Neil Johnson
Roy Charles Johnson
Shane Johnson
Trevor Johnson
William Johnson
Duncan Johnstone
Carl Joice
Ashley Jones
Barry Jones
Norman Dogmeat Jones
Peter Jones
Phil Jones
Paul Jordan
Shaun Jupp
Roger Justice
Alfie Keeler
Mr Lynn Kelly
Paul Kelly
Chris Kemp
Joseph Kempster
Mr G Kench
Marcus Kennedy
Percy Kent

Steve Kent
Alan Kercher
David Ronald Kerr
Mark Peter Kerridge
Marcus Kerridge-Mccoll
Reece Kerridge-Mccoll
Kevin & Philippa
Bradley Kidby
Paul Kidby
Sharon Kilmartin-Bone
Ernest Kimber
Andy King
Barry King
Daniel King
Darren J King
Dave King
Andy Kinnear
George Kinney
David 'Fish' Kingswell
Mark Kirby
Gary Kirton
Grandad Bob Kneller
Kevin M Knight
Laurance Knight
Matthew Knight
Shane Allen Knight
Stephen Knight
Steve Knight
Keith Knipe
Phil Knipe
Paul Knott
John Kruk
Steve Lambert
Peter Lamb-Symon
Ian Laming
Ted Lamont
Ali Lance
Mark Langford
Peter Langridge
Bob Larcombe
Jessica Large
Simon, Oliver & Luke Lashley
Lee Laver
Greg Laver-Baker
Kevin Laverick
Mark Laverick
David Law
Diane Lay
Reg Layton
Stuart Layton
Paul Leclercq
Barbara-Anne Lee
George Lee
Michael Lee
Peter Lee
Jeff Legg
Stephen Leigh
Brian Levison
Tim Lewis
Laura Lidbetter
Archie Light
George Light

Robert Lilly
David Lillywhite
Ian And Daniel Limb - We
Were There
Michael Limburn
Richard Link
Norman Littlefield
Colin Lloyd
Endre Lock
Mark Lockwood (Locky)
Bob Lomas
Allan Long
David Long
Michael Long
Pompey Dan' Longhurst
Sarah Longley
Peter Longyear
Martin Loveridge
Glenn Howard Lucas
Simon & Patricia Lush
Royce Lye
Charles Mack
Wayne Mack
Ewan Mackenzie
Sophia Mackney
Joy Maddox
Joe Magee
Roy Magee
John Maginnis
Gary And Lesley Magor
Paul Major
Julie Malzard
Andy, Sarah And Daniel Mann
Paul & Daniel Mardlin
Darren Bernard Marshall
Ben Martin
Chris & Ollie Martin
Ian Martin
Peter Martin
Ray Martin
Roger Martin
Andy Martindale
Richard Marwood
Dean Maskell
Mark Mason
Alan, Adam Massey
Keiran Massey
Danny & Stanley Mather
Kirk Matthews
Lynne Maund
Maureen
Le May
Russell Maylum
Tony Mcbride
Michael Mccall
Chris, Cheryl, Toby & Jacob
Mccauley
Janet Mccaw
Darin Mccloud
David Mcconnell
Mr Sidney E G Mccutcheon
Neil Mcdonald

Phil Voller And Danny
Mcgonagle
Cavan Mcgrath
Glenn Mcguiness
Kurtis Mckinlay
Connor Mcmain
Thomas Peter Mcnally
Barry Mcnie
Matthew Mcqueen
Bob Meaden
Paul John Meaghan
Tania Meaghan
Jay Meech
Tim Meiris
Alan John Meredith
John And Ryan Merrikin
Tom Mew
Jake Meyers
David Middleton
Keith D Middleton
Anthony Miell
Brad Mihell
Calum Miller
Jeff Miller
John T P Miller
Stephen Mills
Steve Mills
Terry Mills
John Millwater
Edan Milner
Steve&Alex Mingay
Richard Minto
William Brian Missing
Graham Mitchell
Adam Moignard
Graeme Moir
Peter Moir
Phil Monk
Philip J Moody
Colin Moore
Graham Moore
Yvonne & David Moore
John More
Jon Moreno
David & Win Morey
Steve Morey
Jack Morgan
Alan Morley
Alex Morley
Colin Morris
Angus Morrison
Duncan Morrison
Peter Moseley
Garry Mourne
Mick Moxham
Andrew Paul Mugford
Colin Muller
Leigh Murdoch
Darren Murdy
Jimmy Murray
Glen Mussen
Mick Myers

Katherine Myles
Gavin Nanson
Keith Nash
Simon Nash
The Nash Family
Joanna Nelmes
Peter Neumann
Graham Newcombe
Jim And Hayley Newell
Paul Newell
Gary Newlyn
Jeff & Lesley Newman
Mark Newman
Rodger Newman
Roger Nicholas
Simon Nicholls
Nick
Jo Nobes
Danny Noonan
Dave Norman
Jon Norman
Joshua Norris
Mike Nother
Charlie Ogle
David Old
Keith Oliver
Leonie Jayne Oliver
Leonie Jayne Oliver
Shaun Oliver
Andy O'neill
Nick O'neill
Steve O'neill
Cameron David Orr
Maria O'shaughnessy
Daniel Overton
Max Paddon
Paul Paffett
Carl John Page
Malcolm Page
Patrick Page
John Paice
Craig Paintin
Lorraine Paintin
Michael Paintin
Chris Palmer
George Frederick Palmer
Glenys Palmer
Mike Palmer
Vaughan Ivor Palmer
Howard Parke
John & Barbie Parkyn
Paul Patmore
Alan Paz Parrott
Andrew And Harry Parsons
Elaine Parsons
John Parsons
Jason Paskins
Frank Patmore
Mark,Kirsty,Calle,Hayden
Patterson
Steve Patterson
Perry Pattison

Geoff Paul
Chris Pauley
Alli Payne
Jake Payne
Mark Payne
John W Peacham
Ian Peake
Jack Francis Pearce
Mr Peter Pearce
Wendy Pearce
John Pearson
Clive Penney
Kevin Penny
Nigel Perfect
Peter, Phil & Matthew
Luke Peters
Derek Pether
Brian Petracca
Ashton Elijah Pettit
Ethan Oliver Pettit
John Pettitt
Rudi Pfeiffer
Kim Phillips
Phil Phillips
Lezley Picton
Barry Pike
Graham Pindar
Ian Pink
Matt Pitt
Nathan Pitt
Paul Pitt
Robert Pleace
Olivia Ponsford
Steve Pope
Simon Potterton
David J Poulton
Steve And Brody Poulton
Blake Powell
Grandad Steve Powell
Louis & Dan Powell
Nick Powell
William Powell
Tim Poynton
Nigel Pragnell
Clive Prescott
Mike Presswell
Alan Price
Bob Price
Debby & Warren Priestley
Ken Prior
David Prismall 1936 - 2000
Brian Geoffrey Privett
Bob Prowting
Ben Pryke
George Pullen
Chris Purnell
George Purnell
Joel Barreiros Putnam
Chris Quinell,
Pompeydownunder
Phil Quinell
John F Quinn

Pete Radford
David J Raggett
Gemma Louise Raggett
Andy Rain
David Rainer
Gary Ralls
Pat Ralph
Dave Randall
Ian Randall
Jack Randall
Michael Rankine
Kev Ratcliffe
Tim Ratcliffe
Theo Rattue
Leigh Rawlins
Alan John Ray
Jordan Rayment
Andrew Read
Paul Read
Paul Rearn
Tony Redding
John Redgate
Harry Redman
Peter Redman
Ray Reed
Ian Reedy
Dan Rees
Simon David Reeves
Suzanne Reeves
Pete Rennie
Bernie Renyard
Alan Scot Revy
Alexander Rex
Robert Reynolds
Roy Reynolds
John Rice
Kevin Richardson
Paul Richardson
Stuart Richardson
Tony Richardson
Sam Riches
Adam Rickards
Joel Rickards
Neil Rimmington
Ian Risebrough
Kenneth William Ritty
Shaun Robbins
Charlie Roberts And His
Grandma
Mark Roberts
Mark Roberts
Nicky Roberts
Keith Robertson
Alan Robinson
Lewis G Robinson
Paul Robinson
Ric Robinson
Wesley Robinson
Roger And Dorothy
Edward Rolfe
Steve Rolls
Paul Roose (Pompey Paul)

Ian Roper
Gary Rose
Rosemary And Ken
Eddy Ross
Carl Rossiter
Wendy Rouse
Andy & Chris Rowe
John Michael Frederick Rowe
Nigel & Luise Rowe
Charles Roy
Simon Rule
Graham Russell
Cliff Ruston
Bradley Salmon
Tony Salt
Darrell Luke Salter
Georgia Samphire
Graham Sampson
Ciarrai Samson
John Samson
Kirsty Samson
Tim Sanders
Brooke Sanderson
Philip Sandys
Rosemarie & Cyril Saunders
Steve Scanlan
Dean, Donna, Kirsty & Jamie
Scopes
Andy Scott
Frankie Scott
Paul Scott
Brad Seall
Stephen Seall
Derek Searle
Luke Sears
Corinna Seckington
The Sell Family
Terry Sells
John Sexstone
Paul Sexstone
Mike Shaddick
Kieran Sharley
Andrew Shaw
Colin Shaw
David William Shaw
Jayson Shaw
Kelvin Shaw
Darrell Shawyer
Scott Shawyer
Martin & Baby Sheaf
Gary Shepard
Daniel Shepherd
Brett Shepperd
Derek And Andrew Shewring
Shiner
Daniel And Charlie Shipp
Garry And Shirley Shipp
Mike Shipp
Jim Sholl
Mark Sholl
Ken Sim
David Owen Simmons

Luke Simmons
Scott Simmons
Craig Simpson
Ian Skidmore
David Skinner
Cameron Mark Slater
Gary Slight
Mark&Gary&Steve Slight
Jim Smalley
Steve Smethurst
Barry Smith
Callum Smith
Connor Smith
Derek Smith
Emma Smith
Graham Smith
Irene G Smith
Jeff Smith
Kerry Smith
Kevin J Smith
Lee Smith
Mark D Smith
Martin Smith
Neil Smith
Roger Smith
Toby Smith
Ryan Smout
Ben Snook
Nigel Soal
Alan Soffe
Carly Ann Soffe
Aaron Southgate
Paul Southgate
Melvyn Spanner
Val Sparks
Andrew Spencer
Pete Spillett
Thomas Sprake
James Spurgeon
Paul Stallard
Andy Stamp
Jake Squibb
John Stamp
Paul Stamp
Terry Stamp
Toptopdad Lou Stamp
Toptopson Luke Stamp
Steve Stanhope
Commodore David Steele
Megan-Louise Steer
Michael Stenton
Owen Stenton
Stuart Stenton
Robert Stephen
Craig Stevens
Franklin K Stevens
Lee Stevens
Luke Stevens
Nick Stevens
Spencer Stevens
Ham Stewart
Peter Stockdale

Lee Stone
Gavin Stopford
Ken Strange
Matthew Street
David Strong
Neil Strong
Frank Strugnell
Stuart
Bill Stubbington
Allison, Nigel, Samuel And
Oliver Sturt
Ben And Tom Sturt
Tony Stuttaford
Lewis Sudbury
Paul Summers
Bradley Sunderland
Emma Sunderland
James Sunderland
Jonathan Sunderland
Ben, Paul Surry
Brett J Sutton
Allan 'Swannie' Swan
Gary Swatton
Brian Sweeny
Robert Sweeny
Peter Swift
Oliver Taviner
Ross Taviner
Scott Taviner
Brandon Taylor
Chris And Charlie Taylor
Christopher Taylor
Fred Taylor
Ken & Ruth Taylor
Stephen Anthony Taylor
Steve & Ollie Taylor
Elliott Terry
Richard Terry
Adam Thomas
Ben Thomas
Matthew Thomas
Ben Thompson
David Thompson
Peter Thompson
John Robert Thornhill
Michael David Thornhill
Brian Thumwood
Graham John Tidy
Sue Till
Bob Tiller
Adrian J Timms
Adrian John Timms
David Paul Timms
Andrew Tizzard
Alan, Andy And Beccy Todd
Adrian Tolliday
Christopher Tomes
James B Tong
James L Tong
Dan Toone
Dave Topliss
James Tott

Richard Tovery
Albert George Town
Charlie Milan Town
Kelly Anne Town
Kevin Paul Town
Rosie Joyce Town
Gareth Tracey
Richard Tracey
Tracey
Billy Traviss
Ben Treend
Brian C Tregenna
Simon C Tregenna
Dean Treleaven
John & Dean Treleaven
Susan Tremlett
Nigel Tresidder
Kev Trippick
Dave Tropman
Gerry Trott
Peter John Tucker
Raymond Tuckwell
Alan Tulett
Elliott Glenn Keith Turnbull
Glenn Turnbull
Mckenna Burton Turner
Phill Tye
Jack Udy
Gary Underwood
Grant Usher
Paul Usher
Phillip Vaughan
Chris Vickers
Mary Vickers
Michelle Vickers
Craig & Brigitte Vince
Peter Vine
Mark Vinter
Malcolm Voller
Colin Vowles
Ron Waddilove
Simon Waddilove
Matthew Walker
Tony Wall
Jamie Wallace
Michael John Wallace
John Wallin
The Walsh Boys
Andy Walshe
Jo Walters
Barry Warburton
David Warburton
Brian Ward
Gary Ward
Keith Ward
Mike Ward
Steve Ward
Clarry Wardale
Rob Wardale
John Ware
Robert Warne
Darren Warnes

David Wateridge
Shirley Wateridge
Daniel Waterman
Tizzy & Peter Waters
Peter Watters
Liam Thomas Watts
Colin Way
Doug Wearn
Keith Wearn
Russell Wearn
Sam Wearn
Philip Wearne
James & Lucas Webb
Linda & Tanya Webb
Martin Webb
Pete Webb
Robin Webb
Simon Webb
Michael Webster
Alan Welch
Simon Welch
Andy Welsh
Jacqueline Milton Welsh
West Family
Colin Westerby
James Westerby
Martyn Westerby
Rachel Westerby
Sam Westerby
John A Portsmouth Football
Club Westwood
Calum Wharton
Kelvin Whatley
Nigel Wheeler
Darren Whellams
Mr J C Whettem
Keri Whitcher
Mark Whitcher
Bernie White
Brian White
Colin White
Darryl White
Graham White
Heather White
Ian John White
Kev White
Martin Raymond White
Paul Whiteaway
Percy Whitefield
Andrew Whitehorn
Jim Whitmarsh
Peter & Jan Whittaker
Sam Whitter
Christine Whittle
Jordan Wicks
Paul Wiggett
Matthew Wigman
Peter Wigmore
Sue Wilcox
Matt 'Wilko' Wilkie
Grahame, Liam & Ryan Wilkins
John Phillip Wilkins

Andi Williams
Jamie Williams
Paul Williams
Scott Williams
Tony Williams
Trevor Williams
Bert Williamson
Gary Williamson
George Williamson
Greg Williamson
Ian Williamson
Paul Williams
Susie Williamson
Mark Willifer
John Willis
Peter H Willis
Martin Williams
Adam Willsher
Mark Wilson
Richard Wilson
Robyn Wilson
Bill Wiltshire
Steve Windebank
Basil Wingate
Bill Wingate
Kenneth Wingate
Diana Winsor
Perry Winsor
Peter G Winter
Tom Wiseman
Alan Wiseman
Ian Withall
Alex Wood
Pete And Charlotte Wood
Sam Wood
Glenn Woodage
Steve Woodage
Ashley Woodforth
Iain Woodrow
David James Woodward
Mark Wooldridge
Bob Woolley
Jamie Worrall
Joe Worrall
Ella Worthy
John Wragg
David, Natalie And Emily
Wright
Mathew Wright
Victoria Wright
Nigel Wylie
Josh Yard
Karen Yeldon
Ann Young
Christopher Young
James Young
Peter Young
Robert Young
Simon And Adam Young
Warren Young
Harry Yoxall
Jamie Zincke